Extensive Reading

Richard Day
Jennifer Bassett
Bill Bowler
Sue Parminter
Nick Bullard
Mark Furr
Nina Prentice
Minas Mahmood
Daniel Stewart
Thomas Robb

OXFORD
UNIVERSITY PRESS

D1293870

Great Clarendon Street, Oxford, OX2 6DP, United Kingdom

Oxford University Press is a department of the University of Oxford.
It furthers the University's objective of excellence in research, scholarship,
and education by publishing worldwide. Oxford is a registered trade
mark of Oxford University Press in the UK and in certain other countries

First published in 2015

2019 2018 2017

10 9 8 7 6 5 4 3 2

ISBN: 978 0 19 420036 3

Printed in China

This book is printed on paper from certified and well-managed sources

ACKNOWLEDGEMENTS

Back cover photograph: Oxford University Press building/David Fisher.

The publishers would like to thank: Dan Stewart for supplying the photography of
the book cart on page 99, and Oxford Design and Illustrators for resupplying
the artwork on pages 42, 49, 59, 101, 102, 107, and 108.

*Although every effort has been made to trace and contact copyright holders before
publication, this has not been possible in some cases. We apologise for any apparent
infringement of copyright and, if notified, the publisher will be pleased to rectify any
errors or omissions at the earliest possible opportunity.*

Contents

Notes on contributors

Richard Day is Professor in the Department of Second Language Studies, University of Hawaii. He is co-editor of the journal, *Reading in a Foreign Language*, and chairman of the Extensive Reading Foundation. His recent publications include *Cover to Cover* 1–3 (OUP 2009). Dr Day is engaged in a study of the effects of timed-repeated reading on fluency and comprehension.

Jennifer Bassett is the series editor of the Oxford Bookworms Library. For over twenty years she has been writing, editing, and thinking about stories for English language learners. Her publications include about forty original and retold graded readers. Her abiding interests are storytelling within a reduced code, and searching for good stories from every corner of the world.

Bill Bowler and Sue Parminter are freelance ELT authors and teacher trainers based in Alicante, Spain. Since 2000 they have edited the Dominoes series for Oxford University Press. Their other publications include *New Headway Pronunciation* Pre-Intermediate (OUP 2002), and *Happy Earth* new edition (OUP 2009). Their current interests are reader-based drama activities and intensive skills work tasks using graded reader extracts.

Mark Furr has taught in Armenia, Japan, Palau, and the USA. He currently works in Hawaii as an ELT materials writer and editor. He has written journal articles on classroom-based reading groups, and has given presentations and seminars on Reading Circles throughout Japan, the Middle East, and the UK. He is also series editor for the Oxford Bookworms Club: Stories for Reading Circles series.

Nina Prentice is a teacher and teacher trainer with a particular interest in literacy and reading, working in the UK and other countries. She also writes graded readers for Oxford University Press and has just finished *Saladin* for the Dominoes series. She is currently doing research on problems in literary translation.

Minas Mahmood is a senior curriculum specialist in the Bahrain Ministry of Education. She is responsible for secondary-level EFL curriculum renewal. In addition to her interest in teacher development through teacher research, she has been involved with learning and language development in schools through Extensive Reading. She has also contributed to TESOL Arabia's Journal, *Perspectives*.

Daniel Stewart is the Head Foreign Teacher at Kaisei Academy in Tokyo. He has been involved in Extensive Reading since 2002. He is also the editor of the *Extensive Reading Journal* in Japan. His current interests in research include ER, Computer Assisted Language Learning (CALL), and Extensive Listening (EL).

Thomas Robb, PhD, teaches in the Faculty of Foreign Languages, Kyoto Sangyo University, Japan. He is a founding member and past president of the Japan Association for Language Teaching (JALT) and has been involved with the practice and theory of computer use for language learning for over thirty years.

Introduction

Extensive Reading (ER) is becoming an increasingly important component in English language education. Over recent years a wide range of programmes has developed across the world. This growth is no accident, for ER responds to a number of classroom needs.

First, it is an effective way of extending contact with English outside the classroom. Provided appropriately **graded materials** are used, it gives students the opportunity to see the language they learn in a classroom environment used in the context of communicating something – usually a story. And of all the language learning activities that students can do outside the classroom, ER is perhaps the one they are most likely to do, because it can be fun.

Second, it personalizes students' contact with the language. By reading the books that they want to read, at a time and place of their choice, ER both individualizes the learning experience and makes it autonomous. Both of these are features that many of us would wish to introduce into the classroom.

Third, reading and writing have often been neglected in language programmes, despite the fact that many students, for study or work, need to develop both skills. Students can only develop the writing (and reading) skills that they need by reading extensively; writing is not a skill that can develop without models.

Finally, and this point emerges time and time again from the chapters in this book, reading can be pleasurable; and anything that associates language learning with pleasure has great value. Even more than that, it is clear that there are many students who have participated in ER programmes and found the experience life-changing.

In his opening chapter, Richard Day defines ER and looks at some evidence of its success in the classroom. His emphasis on the use of graded materials as an essential part of any programme underlies all of this book – there can be no successful ER without appropriately graded materials.

In the next two chapters, editors of two series of **graded readers** give us their views on how ER materials can be developed and how they see them being used. Jennifer Bassett explains the principles of language grading, stresses the importance of good storytelling, and offers three golden keys to extensive reading – comfort, choice, and enthusiasm. Bill Bowler and Sue Parminter give us some historical background, and look at the development of both graded readers and appropriate support materials.

The next three chapters look at three approaches to ER. Sue Parminter and Bill Bowler look at the use of **class readers** – often the best way of introducing reading into the classroom. Nick Bullard then looks at libraries, including digital libraries, and how they can provide greater choice and diversity of reading for students. And Mark Furr describes the concept of **Reading Circles**, which are classroom-based reading and discussion groups that bring Extensive Reading materials into the classroom as core texts for discussion.

The final section of this book introduces five case studies, and these should prove a valuable resource for those who want to embark on an ERP. They look at some of the obstacles and show how these can be surmounted. Nina Prentice in Jordan and Minas Mahmood in Bahrain describe how an ERP can be introduced successfully in government schools. It is clear in these two programmes that the effect on some students has been profound. Daniel Stewart in a private school and Thomas Robb in a university, both in Japan, describe how a programme can be organized within a single institution. They also outline some elegant solutions to the difficulties they encountered. Nina Prentice then describes a class library project in Italian primary and secondary schools which focuses on learner choice and autonomy to motivate students to acquire both reading and lifelong learning skills.

Two series editors, three approaches to ER, and five case studies of programmes in action – for those who want to introduce ER into their classroom, this book provides the logic for doing so, some possible approaches, and some fine examples of programmes in action.

There are sometimes divergent views or differences in emphasis between the contributions to this volume. This in itself is no bad thing. There is no single ideal approach to ER which fits with every class or every teacher. Teachers need to evaluate these different approaches and judge for themselves what will work best in their own classroom.

Part 1 Extensive Reading: the theory

1 Extensive Reading: the background

Richard Day

Extensive Reading (ER) in the EFL/ESL context is an approach to teaching reading whose goal is to get students reading in the English language and enjoying it. ER is based on the well-established principle that we learn to read by reading. This is true for learning to read our first language as well as foreign languages. In teaching foreign language reading, an ER approach allows students to read, read, and read.

In ER, students read large quantities of easy material (usually books) in English. They read for overall meaning, for information, and for pleasure and enjoyment. Students select their own books, and are encouraged to stop reading if a book is not interesting to them or is too hard; they are also encouraged to expand their **reading comfort zone** (the range of materials that students can read easily and with confidence).

In *Extensive Reading Activities for Teaching Language*, Bamford and Day maintain that an ER approach consists of ten principles. Let us look at the first four:

1 The reading material is easy.

For ER to be possible and for it to have the desired results, learners must read books and other materials that are well within their reading comfort zone. When students do this, they are able to read for overall meaning easily and they don't have to worry about a lot of difficult or unknown words. In helping beginning readers to select what to read, I believe that more than one or two unknown words per page might make the text too difficult for overall understanding for beginning readers. For intermediate learners, appropriate reading material has no more than three or four unknown or difficult words per page. In their article 'Unknown vocabulary density and reading comprehension' in *Reading in a Foreign Language*, Hu and Nation (2000) suggest that learners need to know at least 98 per cent of the words in a book of fiction to be able to read without using their dictionaries.

I recognize that not everyone agrees with using easy materials. Some teachers believe that learners must read difficult texts; they also believe that students need to be challenged when learning to read. Perhaps they think that reading difficult texts helps prepare their students to read materials written for first-language (**L1**) reading.

I believe this confuses the means with the end. Clearly our ultimate goal in teaching students to read is to have them read material written for native readers. But we should not start with that goal! We need to start with books and materials that have been especially written for beginning and intermediate levels of reading ability. Learners have to read texts that they find easy and enjoyable as they learn to read, or they will simply not read at all.

2 **A variety of reading material on a wide range of topics must be available.**
For an Extensive Reading Programme (ERP) to succeed, students have to read. This means that we have to have available a large number of books on a wide variety of topics that appeal to all students. An ER library needs to include books (both fiction and non-fiction), magazines, and newspapers. These should be a mixture of informative books and entertaining magazines and books.

When students read a wide variety of reading material, they learn a flexible approach to reading. They begin to read for different reasons (entertainment, information) and, as a result, begin to read in different ways (**skimming**, **scanning**, more careful reading).

3 **Learners choose what they want to read.**
The key to ER is to allow students to select what they want to read. The principle of student self-selection is related to the fundamental concept of ER: we learn to read by reading. Students are more likely to read material they are interested in. So it makes sense for them to choose what (and where and when) to read.

In addition, students should also be free to stop reading anything that they don't find interesting or which is outside their reading comfort zones, and thus too difficult for overall understanding.

4 **Learners read as much as possible.**
The most crucial element in learning to read is the amount of time students actually spend reading. You have to make sure that your students are given the opportunities to read, and read, and read. This is the 'extensive' element of ER, made possible by the first three principles.

How much should our students read?

The short answer is, as much as possible. I usually set **reading targets** for my students. For example, for beginning EFL readers, the minimum is one book a week. This is realistic, since **language learner literature** (LLL) in the form of **graded readers** for beginners, are necessarily short. Some teachers set their reading targets in terms of time, asking their students to read for 60 minutes a week.

When I observe EFL reading classes, I often find that there is too much 'teacher talk'. When the teacher is talking, the students are not reading. So it is extremely important to give your students enough time in class to read. And while your students are reading, you should be reading too, to set an example. This brings us to Day and Bamford's tenth principle:

10 The teacher is a role model.

This means that we, as teachers, need to read to show our students that we value reading. Our actions have an enormous impact on our students. Students forget what we have taught them, but they remember for a long time our behaviour in the classroom. Teachers who are readers and share with their students their love of reading influence their students. We are not just teaching reading, we are selling it! So when students are reading extensively in class, you need to be doing the same thing.

What are the differences between Extensive Reading and Intensive Reading?

We can compare Extensive Reading to **Intensive Reading** (IR). There are three approaches to teaching IR:

1 grammar translation
2 comprehension questions and language analysis
3 comprehension work and strategies.

In the first approach (grammar translation), students translate short, often difficult reading passages into their mother tongue. Then they study the passage for grammar rules. Learners read aloud and translate. In grammar translation, the meaning of a reading passage is at the word- and sentence-level. A sentence is not regarded as 'meaningful' until it is translated into the students' first language. This approach undoubtedly helps students translate from English into their first language. But it does not help them to learn to read English. Translation is different from reading – translation is not reading, and reading is not translation.

The result of this approach is that students may end up thinking that reading in English means translating and studying grammar. So the chances are that they don't read unless they are forced to do so in the classroom.

In the second approach (comprehension questions and language analysis), students also read short, difficult reading passages and answer a number of comprehension questions to check their literal understanding. They then analyse the reading for certain grammatical structures (for example, simple past tense or *Wh*-questions). This approach may help students to pass entrance examinations. But it presents a serious problem, in that students tend to think that reading is another way of studying English grammar. Moreover, they then don't read enough to help them learn to read.

In the third IR approach (comprehension work and strategies), students read short passages and answer comprehension questions, again, to check their literal understanding. They are then taught various comprehension strategies, for example, finding main ideas, recognizing points of view, etc. They may also have to do vocabulary activities and exercises, such as matching a definition with words from the reading passage.

Unfortunately, with this approach to 'helping' students learn to read, they don't read enough. The fact is that we learn to read by reading.

There is another problem with this IR approach: it confuses learning to read with reading to learn. In general, reading strategies help us when we read to learn; but they really are not much help when students are learning to read.

Finally, we know from research that students learn reading comprehension strategies best when they have at least an intermediate level of reading ability so they can start reading to learn.

Table 1.1 compares ER with IR. From this you can see that there are many critical differences between these two approaches to learning to read.

Extensive Reading	Intensive Reading
Overall understanding	100% understanding
Read a lot	Limited reading
Easy texts	Difficult texts
Fluent reading	Word-for-word reading
Read for meaning in English	Translate into first language
No direct study of grammar	Focus on grammar use and rules
No comprehension questions	Many comprehension questions
No direct teaching of strategies	Direct teaching of strategies
Ignore unknown words	Use dictionaries

TABLE 1.1   *Comparing Extensive Reading and Intensive Reading*

↓ THE CONTRIBUTION OF ER TO LANGUAGE LEARNING

Good things happen when EFL students read extensively in English. Reading a large amount of easy material helps them learn to read – students learn to read by reading, not by translating, studying grammar, or acquiring learning strategies.

ER also helps students move away from a word-by-word approach to reading. It helps them to look for the general meaning of what they read. They can ignore any details they do not fully understand.

Finally, by reading the same patterns of letters, words, and combinations of words again and again, students process them more quickly and accurately and thus develop a **sight vocabulary** (words that are recognized automatically). As a result, they increase their reading speed and

Extensive reading: the background

confidence, and are able to give more attention to working out the meaning of what they are reading.

But there is yet more to ER. There is a large and robust body of literature in scholarly journals that reports the results of research into the impact of ER on learning English in both second language and foreign language contexts. The research has looked at both language learning and the affective dimension of language learning – primarily attitude and motivation. Here is what we know from the research on ER. Studies show that students improve in the following areas:

- vocabulary range and knowledge – they learn a lot of new words and expand their understanding of words they knew before
- writing skills – they become better writers
- positive motivation – they want to learn English
- attitude – they like learning English
- speaking proficiency – they become better speakers of English
- listening proficiency – they understand spoken English better
- grammar – they gain a better knowledge of English grammar.

Table 1.2 opposite is an overview of representative studies conducted in both ESL and EFL environments with diverse populations, from young children to adults.

First, let us look at learning to read. As we might expect, the studies convincingly demonstrate that learners who engage in ER will become better readers in English. Not only does reading comprehension improve, but students who read extensively learn reading strategies without studying them directly.

Second, the research also shows that students are able to increase their **reading rates**. Increasing reading rate is important because rate is a critical component of fluent reading. We know from research that fluent readers are better readers (they score higher on measures of reading comprehension) than slow readers. The results displayed in Table 1.2 are strong confirmation of the benefits of ER on learning to read.

Third, the gains in motivation and attitude (often called **affect**) are equally impressive. Study after study shows how students' attitudes changed toward reading in English and how they became eager readers. In an article in the journal *Language Learning*, Elley reported that the students developed 'very positive attitudes toward books as they raised their literacy levels in English'.

Fourth, in addition to gains in affect and reading proficiency, research demonstrates that students who read extensively also make gains in overall language proficiency. For example, Cho and Krashen reported in 1994 that the four adult ESL case study subjects increased their competence in both listening and speaking abilities.

Fifth, students' writing proficiency is also impacted by reading extensively. This is true at all levels, from primary to university.

Finally, the research convincingly shows that ER increases vocabulary range and knowledge. One of the primary ways in which vocabulary is learned is through reading. Learners encounter the same words over and over again in context, and this results in vocabulary learning.

These benefits of ER happen indirectly. Without directly studying writing, students learn to write better. Without studying vocabulary, they learn words. But perhaps the best result of ER is that students enjoy reading and learning English and want to read more.

Study	Population	Results
Iwahori 2008	EFL, secondary, Japan	Increase in reading rate and general language proficiency
Nishono 2007	EFL, secondary, Japan	Increase in reading strategies and motivation
Horst 2005	ESL, adults, Canada	Increase in vocabulary
Kusanagi 2004	EFL, adults, Japan	Increase in reading rate
Taguchi et al. 2004	EFL, adults, Japan	Increase in reading rate
Sheu 2003	EFL, junior high school, Taiwan	Increase in general language proficiency
Asraf and Ahmad 2003	EFL, middle school, Malaysia	Increase in attitude
Takase 2003	EFL, secondary, Japan	Increase in motivation
Bell 2001	EFL, university, Yemen	Increase in reading rate and general language proficiency
Mason and Krashen 1997	EFL, university, Japan	Increase in writing proficiency
Masuhara et al. 1996	EFL, university, Japan	Increase in reading proficiency and rate
Cho and Krashen 1994	ESL, adults, USA	Increase in reading proficiency, oral fluency, vocabulary, and attitude and motivation
Lai 1993a, 1993b	EFL, secondary, Hong Kong	Increase in reading proficiency and vocabulary
Elley 1991	EFL, primary, Singapore	Increase in reading proficiency and attitude and motivation
Hafiz and Tudor 1990	EFL, primary, Pakistan	Increase in writing proficiency and vocabulary
Robb and Susser 1989	EFL, university, Japan	Increase in reading proficiency and attitude
Pitts, White, and Krashen, 1989	ESL, adults, USA	Increase in vocabulary
Janopoulos 1986	EFL, university, USA	Increase in writing proficiency
Elley and Mangubhai 1981	EFL, primary, Fiji	Increases in reading proficiency and general language proficiency including listening and writing; increase in attitude and motivation

TABLE 1.2   *Results of studies of the benefits of ER on EFL and ESL learners*

Extensive reading: the background

The best material for beginning and intermediate readers is language learner literature (materials such as graded readers) specifically written for language learners. Materials are the heart and soul of an Extensive Reading Programme (ERP). Make sure your students have a wide variety of interesting books and materials. In addition to selecting high-interest materials, try to ensure a wide variety of different genres of books, because students' tastes in reading also vary greatly. For example, some students might want to read mystery or detective stories while others might enjoy reading romance or science fiction. Others might be attracted to non-fiction, such as biography.

For most learners of English, by far the most suitable reading materials are books, magazines, and newspapers especially written for EFL learners. This language learner literature is published in increasing quantity, variety, and sophistication by both local and global publishers. There are hundreds of attractive fiction and non-fiction graded readers available and appropriate for students of different ages and interests. These include folk tales, science fiction, thrillers adapted from best-selling authors, classics, travel guides, and novels based on popular films or television shows.

Oxford University Press has an excellent selection of graded readers, The Oxford Bookworms Library. Bookworms Starters provide the ideal foundation for learning to read in English, with a selection of stories written in the present tense and using no more than 250 **headwords**. They are published in three lively formats: Comic Strip, Narrative, and Interactive. Oxford's Bookworms Library offers a huge choice of carefully graded titles featuring modern fiction, **adaptations** of classics, play scripts, and factual texts to engage interest at every level from beginner to advanced.

Unfortunately, the use of graded readers in EFL is controversial, because some believe they are not authentic. A number of experts and teachers claim that students should read only authentic materials.

One reason for using authentic materials to teach reading is that they reflect real-world goals. In an article in the *ELT Journal*, Wong, Kwok, and Choi claim:

> In particular, authentic materials can help us to achieve the aims of enriching students' experiences in the learning and use of English, sensitizing them to the use of English in the real world, and helping them to generate a learning strategy for learning not only English but also other subjects.

However, the supporters of this argument offer no evidence for their views. It is my position that the reason given (that teachers should use authentic materials because they prepare students for the world outside the classroom) is unwarranted. I believe that this reason confuses the goal with the means, confusing the desired outcome (language learning and teaching) with the process of achieving this outcome.

Finally, this reason for using authentic materials (to expose them to the real world outside the classroom) again confuses learning to read with reading to learn. Students first need to learn to read. When they have learned to read, then they can read to learn about the world of English outside their classrooms.

Another criticism of graded readers is that they are not only not authentic, but simplified. This means, the critics claim, that they are poorly written, uninteresting, and hard to read. Moreover, critics argue that graded readers lack normal text features such as **redundancy** and **cohesion**. In addition, because the language of graded readers is adapted to students' language levels, they are regarded as poor models for students.

These criticisms of adapted materials are not valid. Of course there are poorly written and uninteresting graded readers. But equally there are also poorly written and uninteresting authentic materials. To put it another way, just because a book is authentic does not automatically mean that it is well written.

Given that not everyone agrees on using or not using graded readers, let us now look at the use of authentic materials (materials written for first-language readers) to teach reading. The biggest problem here is that authentic materials are too difficult for beginning and intermediate readers, and for this reason they create problems. The first is that a difficult book forces the reader to focus on the **linguistic code** and not on the meaning. As a result, students spend their valuable time and energy decoding the words and using their dictionaries. This means that they are not learning to read and to enjoy reading in the foreign language.

Another problem with using authentic materials to teach reading is that because these are too difficult, students quickly become discouraged. They may feel that learning to read is too hard and so give up.

Using authentic texts that are too difficult for most language learners, is a little like learning to play the piano. Learners start with easy pieces. Teachers do not ask their pupils to move straight on to music by Beethoven, Mozart, or Liszt. In order to reach that goal, beginners start at the beginning by learning to play music written for beginners.

Similarly, in teaching reading, you need to let your students read material appropriate for their reading abilities and level. We need to put the issue of authentic materials aside and think instead of materials appropriate for the students' abilities and the goals of the curriculum, the course, and the lesson.

'Appropriate materials' in this context generally means graded readers. These have the vocabulary, **syntax**, length, and complexity suited to a particular grade (or level or stage). The vocabulary used in graded readers is determined primarily by frequency of occurrence. This means that the lower levels of graded readers will use the most frequent words in English. The higher levels of graded readers will use all the words found in the lower levels and, in addition, other, less frequent words.

Another characteristic of graded readers is appropriate syntax: the beginning levels contain easy syntax, while higher levels use more complex structures. In addition to appropriate vocabulary and syntax, the length of graded readers must also be appropriate to the level – the lower the grade, the shorter the graded reader. Graded readers written for beginners may be limited to 10–15 pages, with many illustrations to help

Extensive reading: the background

convey meaning. Those for advanced learners may reach 80–100 pages with few, if any, illustrations.

Graded readers must also be appropriate in their degree of complexity. For example, the plot of a graded reader novel written for beginners (for example, a starter level) would not be as complex as the plot of a graded reader novel written for advanced learners (a level 6). In addition, in the starter graded reader, there would not be as many characters as in the level 6 novel.

Finally, graded readers are appropriate for an ERP, because, like the Oxford University Press Bookworms Library, they cover a wide variety of genres, from fiction to biography to stage plays to factual texts. This meets Day and Bamford's second principle, discussed earlier:

2 **A variety of reading material on a wide range of topics must be available.**

Graded readers are, after all, written for a very wide range of ages and tastes.

What should students do after reading a book?

The easy answer is that they should choose another easy and interesting book and read it. And do this again and again – remember that we learn to read by reading.

After reading, students may be asked to carry out ER activities based on the books they have read. Not everyone agrees with this. Some feel that students should spend all their time reading books and not doing activities. I do not agree with this.

In my teaching, I like to use ER activities for several reasons.

The first reason is that it helps me to monitor my students' reading. Because most of the reading is done outside the classroom, I cannot actually see my students reading. When they do activities based on their books, I know that they are or have been reading. They cannot do the activities if they have not read the books!

A second reason for doing ER activities is that they can be fun. Students often enjoy them, and this helps to confirm that learning to read can be enjoyable.

A third reason is that activities can help students with developing other skills in English. For example, after reading a book, students could do a writing activity based on their books. There are many types of activities designed to improve reading, oral fluency, vocabulary, and literature. In *Extensive Reading Activities for Teaching Language*, Bamford and Day suggest more than 100 ER activities.

 *Getting it right*

Regular after-reading activities

Suggest a regular time for ER and ER activities. Students enjoy these activities. But if they have not read their books, they will not be able to do the activities.

Try this ☞　**A sample after-reading activity**

One such activity is 'The gift' (Reiss 2004). Students write about the gifts that they would like to give the characters in their books. This is much more exciting and interesting than writing book reports (which students dislike writing and teachers dislike reading).

↓ HOW DOES AN EXTENSIVE READING PROGRAMME WORK?

ER can be incorporated into any EFL curriculum, regardless of methodology or approach. For example, programmes based on comprehension work and strategy-training approach can add an ER component without modifying existing goals and objectives. ER complements a curriculum because, while helping the programme to achieve its objectives of teaching students to read and pass examinations, it broadens those objectives and improves students' attitude toward achieving them.

ER supports all aspects of an English-language programme. As Davis (1995) puts it:

> Any ESL, EFL, or L1 classroom will be poorer for the lack of an extensive reading program of some kind, and will be unable to promote its pupils' language development in all aspects as effectively as if such a programme were present.

There are at least four ways you could integrate ER into your EFL or ESL curriculum. They are:

- create a new course – this would be solely ER
- add to an existing course – this could be any type of course (for example, four skills, grammar, reading)
- incorporate ER into an after-school club – students would get together to read books on a regular basis (say, twice a month)
- read during the homeroom period – students select and read books during their homeroom time.

Let us look at the second way – adding ER to an existing course. When ER is added to a course, nothing is taken away or eliminated from the course. Instead, reading graded readers is simply an addition, an extra requirement of the course.

 **Getting it right**

Set reading targets and give grades

When you incorporate ER into a course, it is important to give the students a grade for the books they read. Set reading targets: let the students know they have to read a certain number of books during the semester (or term) in order to get a certain grade. If the reading target is two books a week for a ten-week term, then the students will have to read 20 books to get the full credit.

Regardless of how you set up your ERP, you will always need to introduce the concept of ER to your students from the start. Day and Bamford explain that students might not understand why they are being asked to read 'easy' books when they are used to reading more difficult texts. So you need to introduce them to the benefits of ER, and to point out that it involves no tests or quizzes.

This is Day and Bamford's ninth principle:

9 Teachers orient and guide their students.

Teachers should also monitor or guide their students through an ERP. For example, students sometimes read on one level, say a beginning level, for too long. If you notice this, you need to encourage them to select books from the next level up.

It is also important to demonstrate the importance of reading in general by creating a regular time for **Sustained Silent Reading** (SSR) in class.

Why this works

One important fact needs repeating: we learn to read by reading. There is no other way. ER is there to help students to become good readers, and you are there to be their guide, coach, and cheerleader in this endeavour.

References

Asraf, R. M. and **I. S. Ahmad.** 2003. 'Promoting English language development and the reading habit among students in rural schools through the Guided Extensive Reading program.' *Reading in a Foreign Language 15/2*: 83–102.

Bamford, J. and **R. R. Day** (Eds.). 2004. *Extensive reading activities for teaching language*. Cambridge: Cambridge Univerisity Press.

Bell, T. 2001. 'Extensive reading: Speed and comprehension.' *The Reading Matrix, 1*. Retrieved October 28, 2006. (See 'Useful websites' on page 112. Site accessed October 28, 2006.)

Cho, K. and **S. D. Krashen.** 1994. 'Acquisition of vocabulary from the Sweet Valley Kids series: Adult ESL acquisition.' *Journal of Reading 37*: 662–7.

Davis, C. 1995. 'Extensive reading: an expensive extravagance?' *ELT Journal 49*: 329–36.

Day, R. R. and **J. Bamford.** 2002. 'Top ten principles for teaching extensive reading.' *Reading in a Foreign Language 14/2*. (See 'Useful websites' on page 112.)

Elley, W. B. 1991. 'Acquiring literacy in a second language: The effect of book-based programs.' *Language Learning 41*.

Elley, W. B. and **F. Mangubhai.** 1981. *The impact of a book flood in Fiji primary schools*. Wellington: New Zealand Council for Educational Research.

Hafiz, F. M. and **I. Tudor.** 1990. 'Graded readers as an input medium in L2 learning.' *System 18*: 31–42.

Horst, M. 2005. 'Learning L2 vocabulary through extensive reading: A measurement study.' *The Canadian Modern Language Review 61*: 355–82.

Hu, M. H. and **P. Nation.** 2000. 'Unknown vocabulary density and reading comprehension.' *Reading in a Foreign Language, 13/1*. (See 'Useful websites' on page 112.)

Iwahori, Y. 2008. 'Developing reading fluency: A study of extensive reading in EFL.' *Reading in a Foreign Language, 20/1*.

Kusanagi, Y. 2004. 'The class report 2: Course evaluation of Pleasure Reading Course.' The Journal of Rikkyo University Language Center 11: 29–42.

Janopoulos, M. 1986. 'The relationship of pleasure reading and second language writing proficiency.' *TESOL Quarterly 20* (4). 763–8.

Lai, F. -K. 1993a. 'Effect of extensive reading on English learning in Hong Kong.' *CUHK Educational Journal 2/1*: 23–36.

Lai, F.-K. 1993b. 'The effect of a summer reading course on reading and writing skills.' *System 21*: 87–100.

Mason, B. and S. D. Krashen. 1997. 'Extensive reading in English as a foreign language.' *System 25*: 91–102.

Masuhara, H., T. Kimura, A. Fukada, and M. Takeuchi. 1996. 'Strategy training or/and extensive reading?' in T. Hickey and J. Williams (eds.) *Language, Education, and Society in a Changing World* (pp. 263–74). Clevedon, UK: Multilingual Matters.

Nishino, T. 2007. 'Beginning to read extensively: A case study with Mako and Fumi.' *Reading in a Foreign Language 19/2*: 76–105.

Pitts, M., H. White, and S. D. Krashen. 1989. 'Acquiring second language vocabulary through reading: A replication of the clockwork orange study using second language acquirers.' *Reading in a Foreign Language 5*: 271–5.

Reiss, P. 2004. 'The gift.' In J. Bamford and R. R. Day (eds.) *Extensive reading activities for teaching language* (pp. 156–57). Cambridge: Cambridge University Press.

Robb, T. N. and B. Susser. 1989. 'Extensive reading vs skills building in an EFL context.' *Reading in a Foreign Language 5*, 239–51.

Sheu, S. P.-H. 2003. 'Extensive reading with EFL learners at beginning level.' *TESL Reporter,' 36*: 8–26.

Taguchi, E., M. Takayasu-Maass, and G. J. Gorsuch. 2004. 'Developing reading fluency in EFL: How assisted repeated reading and extensive reading affect fluency development.' *Reading in a Foreign Language 16*: 1–23.

Takase, A. 2003. 'The effects of extensive reading on the motivation of Japanese high school students.' Unpublished doctoral dissertation. Temple University, Japan.

Wong, V., P. Kwok, and N. Choi. 1995. 'The use of authentic materials at tertiary level.' *ELT Journal 49*: 318–22.

2 A series editor's view (1)

Jennifer Bassett

> I try instantly to set in motion a certain forward tilt of suspense or curiosity, and at the end of the story or novel to rectify the tilt, to complete the motion.[1]
> JOHN UPDIKE

It is this 'certain forward tilt of suspense or curiosity' that lies at the pedagogical heart of **language learner literature** (LLL), or **graded readers**, as they are usually known. Storytelling has been around for a long time. We are narrative animals, and we use storytelling to make sense of the world around us – we organize our experience into narrative form. This is the purpose of graded readers: to bring the language learner, or beginner reader, into the charmed circle of storytelling, where the urge to turn the page, to find out what happens next, takes over. And at the end of the story, when the tilt is rectified, the motion completed, the learner is left with a thirst to repeat the experience, to begin another story, and after that, another …

In this chapter I will try to answer three questions about graded readers:

- What is a graded reader?
- What makes a good graded reader?
- What are graded readers for?

↓ WHAT IS A GRADED READER?

A graded reader is a narrative text written for a particular community of readers, the community of second or foreign language learners. This is a very wide and diverse community, but its members share some common characteristics. They are likely to be slow readers, reluctant readers, unconfident readers, and readers with a limited competence in the target language. This is why the language in graded readers must be controlled, and the stories must be written in language that will be accessible to the learners at their current stage of linguistic competence.

Most series of graded readers will follow a linguistic syllabus of some kind, in which the permitted language for each stage or level in the series is set out in grammar tables and wordlists. The Oxford Bookworms Library series is no exception. There are detailed structural tables and wordlists for each level to guide the writer and editor into using appropriate language for that level. But it is important to point out that this structural and **lexical syllabus** is only a small part of what constitutes language grading. It is the tip of the iceberg, the obvious part above water that everyone can see. But nine-tenths of the iceberg is under water, and is not visible to the naked eye.

Similarly with language grading; it is the part under water that can make all the difference between a text that is readable and accessible, and one that is not.

Lexical grading and headwords

A lexical syllabus, or wordlist, consists of a list of **headwords** which beginner readers are expected to know at each level in a graded reader series. A headword is a word that forms a heading in a dictionary, under which its meaning is explained. Examples of headwords are *go, happy, book*. The 'families' of these words could include the following:

go: goes, going, went, gone
happy: happier, happily, unhappy, happiness
book: books

These derived forms would not be in the headwords list, but they could be used in a text at that level without the need for glossing.

So far, so clear. But English is a language rich in homophones, and the range of denotative and connotative meanings attached to any word can be very wide. There are many traps awaiting the unwary author or editor of graded reading texts. Most wordlists will include the items *go, book, for* at a low level, but what about these meanings and usages?

He was driving home when his brakes went.
Whose go is it?
You're booked on the evening flight.
She does the books for the company.
His face was grim and unsmiling, for he brought bad news.

The beginner reader is unlikely to be familiar with these usages, so the author or editor must take care that these meanings are avoided, or are put into a glossary, or are supported by internal glossing in the narrative. Wordlists are only a rough and ready starting point for lexical grading. Just as important is a sensitivity to the accessibility of the language used and a constant alertness to the difficulties that a beginner reader might experience while negotiating meaning from a text.

In any story there will be vocabulary essential to the topic of the story, but which is outside the wordlist for that level. Wherever possible, the writer should try to provide contextual support for the meaning of these words in the narrative, and they will also be explained in a glossary in the book.

Structural grading and syntax

As with lexical grading, the obvious part of structural grading – the bit of the iceberg above water – is the grammatical syllabus of verb forms, active/passive voice, pronouns, determiners, and so on. These follow the progression of introduction generally found in most coursebooks, in that simple verb forms appear in lower-level texts. Complex modal forms, for example, would not be used until a more advanced level. Where grading becomes less easy to tabulate, however, is the way the discrete grammatical forms combine in a text. Reference, **ellipsis**, embedding, inversion, non-linear progression, and many other features of continuous text can cause difficulties even if the learner is familiar with the grammatical forms. To take the example of embedding, look at these sentences:

> He agreed to marry **a girl his mother** had chosen for him in her own village.
> He wondered **what it was that** she liked about Lairdman.
> All she **does is sit** at a computer all day long.
> The first thing he **did was look** at the engine.

Beginner readers often process a text word by word, so the juxtaposition of two nouns (*a girl his mother*) or three verbs (*does is sit*) can cause them to hesitate and lose the flow of the story. Good language grading will ensure that syntactic features like these are used only with caution and as appropriate for the level. It is also important to keep a balance between descriptive text, which is syntactically much denser, and dialogue, which is usually easier to process.

Accessibility and readability

This last aspect of language grading – the iceberg under water – is the hardest to describe in a paragraph. There are no rules that can be universally applied, as each story must be assessed on its own needs, its own narrative dynamic. But these are the kinds of questions lying at the back of my mind as series editor when I assess a text for language grading:

- How heavy is the information load in descriptive passages? For example, is the language being overworked with too many adjectives, too many adverbs?
- In dialogues, is the reference system clear? How much ellipsis is there?
- Does the narrative have good **cohesion**? Is there appropriate use of link words, **discourse markers**, time shift signals, scene shift signals, **redundancy**?
- Is 'given' and 'new' information used effectively for linking? Is there enough variety in sentence patterns, in front-weighting and end-weighting?
- Above all, are the rhythms right? Does the language ebb and flow in a paragraph? Does it sound and feel right when read aloud? (All writers of fiction should read their work aloud as they write.)

All these linguistic features of continuous text can help carry the beginner reader along through the story on a smooth and uninterrupted journey, as though floating effortlessly downstream on a river. Let us take one small example and look at a sentence from a Stage 1 graded reader:

> 1 Sara went to the shops five or six times a day, and when she walked past the house next door, she often thought about the Indian gentleman. [2]

This is a long sentence, of two coordinated main clauses, linked by a subordinate clause. The progression of ideas in the sentence, however, is linear, moving from given information that the reader already knows (Sara's regular shopping habits), through a time and location marker also containing given information (the house next door), to the new information in the last clause (thinking about the Indian gentleman). Now compare example 1 with the three sentences in example 2:

> 2 Sara went to the shops five or six times a day. She walked past the house next door. She often thought about the Indian gentleman.

These three sentences are much shorter, but are actually much harder for the reader to process because there is no narrative linking, no connection between ideas, and so no forward movement in the language.

Finally, a warning about **readability formulae**. These programmes mostly use the criteria of word length and sentence length to assess readability, and take no account of narrative cohesion or complex syntax. Example 1, for example, will get quite a low score, around 66 on the Flesch Reading Ease scale, simply because of its length. The sentence in example 3 below will be rated as much easier, around 80 on the scale, because it is shorter. The syntax, however, has complex embedding and a beginner reader would find it much harder to process than the longer sentence in example 1.

> 3 All he cared about was changing the way we did it.

Language grading, in all its aspects, is an essential feature in a graded reader, but it is a means to an end, not an end in itself – which leads into my next question.

↓ WHAT MAKES A GOOD GRADED READER?

If we compare a graded reader to a horse and cart, we might say that the language grading and the appearance of the book (attractive cover, illustrations, good typography) are the cart, and the story is the horse. And if you put the cart *before* the horse, we all know what happens – you don't go anywhere. So the horse must come first, the story must have priority. The story is the engine that drives the whole enterprise of **Extensive Reading** (ER).

The key ingredient, then, of a good graded reader is a good story, but what do we mean by a 'good story'? Here is a famous storyteller on the subject:

> The story-maker ... makes a Secondary World which your mind can enter. Inside it, what he relates is 'true': it accords with the laws of that world. You therefore believe, while you are, as it were, inside. The moment disbelief arises, the spell is broken; the magic, or rather art, has failed ...
> J. R. R. TOLKIEN[3]

One way of thinking about stories is to use an analysis from narratology and to make the distinction between *fabula* and *sjuzhet*.

- *Fabula* is the basic story material – the chronological sequence of events that take place in the fictional world.
- *Sjuzhet* is the storytelling, the narrative techniques – plot, framework, narrative voice, narrative clock, viewpoint, focalization – all the artifices used to shape the events into a narrative.

An example of a fabula is *Boy meets girl, boy loses girl, boy finds girl again*. This simple fabula underlies many of the world's love stories, from the classic nineteenth-century novels of Jane Austen to the teen romances of the modern age. The fabula, the basic story material, is often less significant than the sjuzhet, the way the story is told, and the craftsmanship of the writing.

Graded readers are written in easy language, a reduced language code, but good craftsmanship in the storytelling is just as necessary as in any other fiction writing. If a plot is limp and weakly constructed, if characters are two-dimensional and unconvincing, the magic or art that Tolkien talks about will fail, and the spell will be broken. The language of graded readers may be simple, but the storytelling should not be simplistic. Narratives that employ few, if any, of the devices of the storyteller's art will not hold a reader's attention for long. Beginner readers, especially, can quickly lose heart and fail to persevere with a story that does not grip them.

It is not easy to set out guidelines for good storytelling. Each story is its own world. It has its own dynamic, its own pace, creates its own internal laws, uses its own patterns of narrative voice and focalization. To look at one small example, here is an extract from a retelling of a well-known fairy tale, a story that has appeared in many cultures over hundreds of years, retold in version after version … :

> All that evening the Prince danced only with Cinderella. Already, he was deeply in love. 'How beautiful she is!' he thought. 'What a soft, gentle light shines in her eyes!'
>
> When people are happy, time passes very quickly. Now the clock begins to strike the hour of midnight. Hurry, Cinderella, hurry! In a few seconds your fine dress will change back to rags, and you will be once more a little kitchen servant with bare, dirty feet and untidy hair.
>
> Cinderella heard the clock and looked up. 'Oh dear! I have stayed too long,' she thought. 'I must go!'
>
> And away she ran, out of the ballroom, through the palace. But as she ran, one of her glass slippers fell from her foot …[4]

This is a **third-person narrative**, but with limited points of view, and with changes of focalization. First we have the Prince's view of events, then Cinderella's. This switch of focalization has the effect of foregrounding each character and helping the reader to empathize with them. There is also a switch in the second paragraph to an omniscient third-person narrative with an overt narrator, offering reader-friendly exposition whenever it is needed. This is a useful device when writing for beginner readers as it can help them to keep a grip on the information flow. Finally, there is the tense shift in the second paragraph, from the narrative past to the narrative present and back again – a standard device (often used by Charles Dickens) for increasing the tempo and raising the emotional temperature.

Many writers have given good advice on storytelling, some of which is especially relevant to graded readers. The Russian writer Anton Chekhov famously advised a friend:

> If in the first chapter you say that a gun hung on the wall, in the second or third chapter it must without fail be discharged. [5]

In other words, if the narrative creates an expectation in the reader, that expectation must be fulfilled. Or, conversely, if a gun is going to be fired later in the story, that event needs to be foreshadowed by a mention of the gun earlier. Foreshadowing prepares the reader for later events. In the extract from *Cinderella*, it is not a gun hanging on the wall, of course, but a glass slipper falling from a foot ... and we all know what happens to that.

Further excellent advice for writers of graded readers comes from Elmore Leonard:

> Try to leave out the part that readers tend to skip. Think of what you skip reading a novel: thick paragraphs of prose you can see have too many words in them. [6]

Many language learners must have been put off extensive reading by flicking through a book and seeing those 'thick paragraphs of prose' with 'too many words' in them.

Original stories and adaptations

Where do good stories come from? The short answer is, anywhere. They can come from any era, any culture, any source. They may be original stories, or retold stories, that is, **adaptations** of existing novels or short stories. The important question to ask about a graded reader is not where the story came from, but how good is the storytelling, the craftsmanship of the writing.

Some people criticize adaptations, on the grounds that stories retold for language learners are not 'authentic' texts, and are not examples of 'real' English. In Chapter 1, Richard Day explains why authentic materials are not appropriate for beginner readers and shows that the reasons for *not* using graded readers are misguided. I would like to take the discussion of authentic texts a little further. Authenticity, it seems to me, is not a characteristic of text itself, but has to do with the relationship between reader and text.

An adaptation is a story retold for a different community of readers – the same *fabula*, but a different *sjuzhet*. Retelling a novel is like rebuilding a house. First, you take down the house, brick by brick: you take off the roof, take out the doors and the window frames and the staircases; you study the electrical wiring, examine the plumbing, dig up the foundations – you get to know every nook and cranny of the building, everything that makes it work as a dwelling. And when you know all the building materials inside out, then you start to rebuild – but to your own design. Your rooms will be smaller; there will be fewer of them. Your ceilings will be less ornate; your light fittings will have simple lampshades, not vast chandeliers. The internal arrangement of corridors and staircases and connecting doors will be much less complicated, and possibly quite different. But – and here is the key – your windows will have the same outlook, the same view onto the world outside.

A well-written adaptation is a retelling, the creation of a new narrative with its own cohesion and continuity, its own light and shade, its own pace and momentum. The way to judge an adaptation is not to compare it to its source text, but to judge it as a story in its own right, and in its appropriacy for its target readership. These seem to me more useful criteria than questions about whether a text is 'authentic' or not. It also seems more meaningful to approach the question from the reader's point of view:

> People make a text real by realizing it as discourse [...] And this reality does not travel with the text.
> H. G. WIDDOWSON[7]

From this viewpoint authenticity is *achieved* in the process of reading when the reader realizes the intentions of the writer. And that is the whole point of language learner literature – to provide texts which are within the linguistic competence of learners, and so can be authenticated as **discourse**.

Choosing stories for graded readers

How do we choose stories for the Bookworms Library? We read, and read, and read some more. For one volume of World Stories, for example, I might read thirty, forty, or even fifty short stories by different Asian writers, then select a 'longlist' of about fifteen or so stories that I think might work well as adaptations. A World Stories reading panel will then read all the stories on the longlist, and write short reports on them. After much discussion, a shortlist of four or five stories is decided on – and the long journey to a finished Bookworm has finally begun.

Every type of story, every genre, every theme is explored in the search for Bookworms. We look for stories that we hope will resonate with students across cultural boundaries, that have universal themes, whether it is the relationship between children and parents, a romantic love story, the fear of the supernatural, or questions about crime and punishment raised by a detective thriller. Kazuo Ishiguro, a writer with links to two different cultures, puts it like this:

> I am a writer who wishes to write international novels. What is an 'international' novel? I believe it to be one, quite simply, that contains a vision of life that is of importance to people of varied backgrounds around the world. It *may* concern characters who jet across continents, but may just as easily be set firmly in one small locality.[8]

Some people question the presence of darker themes in some stories in a graded reader series, but these are often the stories that will challenge and stimulate readers most. From fiction we can learn what is good and what is bad, what is generous and what is selfish, what is kind and what is cruel. Corruption in governments, child soldiers in Africa, cruelty within a family, betrayal of a friend – young minds may have no direct experience of these things, but after reading stories about them, their moral compass on such subjects will surely be more clearly defined.

Here is a comment, verbatim, from a student after reading *Cries from the Heart: Stories from Around the World*, short stories mainly by African and Asian writers:

> I was lost in thought for a long time after I read all of this stories. I want everyone to read this book. Because this book tells us important things that we should think. Especially, first story "The Photograph" was very shocking. It's the story between hungry and wealth. I learned that we should think not only our life, but also everyone's life in the world. I want all the countries of the world to maintain peace. [9]

A reaction like that, heartfelt and engaged, shows that the purpose of the graded reader has been achieved. Tolkien's magic has not failed.

↓ WHAT ARE GRADED READERS FOR?

Put simply, their purpose is to bring enjoyment and pleasure to the language learner. That is their primary purpose. The secondary purpose, which will only be achieved if the primary purpose is achieved first, is to increase learners' language proficiency through the activity of ER. Much is written elsewhere in this book about the theory, practice, and benefits of ER, but I would like just to propose three golden keys. As a storyteller, I must have three of them, of course, as the 'rule of three' features in so many stories (Aladdin is locked in the cave for three days, Cinderella goes to the ball three times, the hero of a story is given three wishes …).

Comfort

Learners need to feel *comfortable* with the language level, and to read within their own linguistic 'comfort zone'. ER is only effective when students can read with ease and are not distracted by struggles with unknown words and unfamiliar structures. If they find a text too difficult, they should be encouraged to try a lower language level. The purpose of this kind of reading is not to meet new and difficult language, but to develop reading fluency and lifelong reading skills and, above all, to enjoy the experience.

It is important for students (and sometimes also their parents) to realize that easy reading is not *lazy* reading. Research into the neuroscience of the reading brain suggests that the **working memory** plays a key role in the development of reading fluency. Easy reading will encourage pleasure reading, which will lead to more reading; more reading will lead to faster, more fluent reading; and fluent reading will reduce the burden on working memory. This, as Maryanne Wolf describes in *Proust and the Squid* [10], 'gives each new reader time to make predictions, to form new thoughts, to go beyond the text, and to become an independent learner.'

Choice

Not everybody likes the same kinds of story. Some people like ghost stories, some like mysteries, some like love stories, and some prefer real-life stories and non-fiction. The important thing is to make available a wide range of books, at the right language levels, for students to choose from. You, as the teacher, have to step back here, and allow your students a free choice. Self-selected material is far more likely to be motivating, and to lead students into pleasure reading.

Beginner readers may be unsure as to what kind of book they do like, and here you can provide helpful guidance in the process of choice – how to find out about a story from the back-cover blurb, the cover, the illustrations. Above all, students should be aware that it is fine *not* to like a book. If they are not enjoying it or are finding it too difficult, encourage them to put it back and try another.

Enthusiasm

This may be the most important key of all. Teachers who are keen readers themselves, and enthusiastic about books and stories and reading, will be positive role models for their students. Enthusiasm is catching. If you are reading the same books as your students, and are able to share and exchange responses with them on an equal basis, a community of readers can develop that everyone wants to be included in.

Enthusiasm for reading is a delicate flower, however. It can be killed very easily. Many teachers experienced in running **Extensive Reading Programmes** (ERPs) warn of the negative effect on students' motivation to read if, after finishing a book, they are faced with comprehension questions, tests, and demands for summaries. These pedagogical tasks give little scope for the kind of **reader response** that a storyteller like Philip Pullman is hoping for from his readers: 'I love this. It made my heart turn over, I was so happy when I read it.' [11]

The best kind of ER activities are those that encourage reader response, and these, as Richard Day pointed out in Chapter 1, can help teachers monitor their students' reading.

But teachers often ask how to motivate students to read. They don't read for pleasure in their own language, they have no culture of reading. These are valid questions. How can reading compete with the easy charm of the visual media that surround students every day? You cannot *make* someone read.

Perhaps the best advice I have come across is from teachers who focus first, not on the reading, but on the story. Students may be reluctant to read, but who can resist that 'certain forward tilt of suspense or curiosity', the power of a good story to draw you in? Daniel Pennac (*The Rights of the Reader* [12]) reads aloud to his students. He reads 'novels to an audience convinced they don't like reading'. Be patient, he says, and until you have 'patched up your students' relationship with reading', ask for nothing in return. Nothing …

Reading as a gift.
Read and wait.
Curiosity is awakened, not forced.

↓ THE SERIES EDITOR'S ROLE

Comfort, choice, and enthusiasm are my golden keys to extensive reading. Teachers will find different ways of setting up and running ERPs according to the particular needs and circumstances of their own teaching environment. The series editor's role, as I understand it, is to provide learners with an irresistible feast of stories, well-crafted narratives at different language levels that will engage learners' interest and attention, and lead them into the virtuous circle of positive reinforcement. They read one story and find it is an enjoyable experience, so they want to start another, and then another … and in this way, quietly in the background, their language proficiency will be increasing.

Stories are written to entertain, to amuse, to enchant, to horrify, to delight, to make us laugh, to make us cry, to make us wonder, to make us think … . And if, as Philip Pullman has written[13], we forget the true purpose of something, it becomes empty, just a meaningless task. The purpose of what I do as a writer and editor is to delight. I hope that the students who read Bookworms will do so because they enjoy them.

Endnotes

1 John Updike gave useful insights into the novelist's art. This is from an interview he gave in 1968. The Art of Fiction No 43. Interview in *The Paris Review*, Issue 4. (See 'Useful websites on page 112. Site last retrieved 30 May 2010.)

2 From *A Little Princess*, 1998. Frances Hodgson Burnett, retold by Jennifer Bassett. Oxford Bookworms Stage 1. Oxford University Press. p. 24.

3 J. R. R. Tolkien, author of *The Lord of the Rings*, wrote a famous essay 'On Fairy-stories', in *Tree and Leaf* (1964). George Allen & Unwin Ltd.

4 From a retelling of the *Cinderella* story. Jennifer Bassett. Unpublished manuscript.

5 Anton Chekhov, 1927. In S. S. Koteliansky (ed. & tr.), *Anton Tchekhov: literary and theatrical reminiscences*. Quoted in N. J. Lowe, 2000. *The Classical Plot and the Invention of Western Narrative*. Cambridge University Press. p. 25.
This famous piece of advice is Chekhov's metaphor for the linking in the plot, the setting up of a firm network of probable and necessary consequences. Later advice from Raymond Chandler, the creator of the Los Angeles private eye Philip Marlowe, offered an ironic variant to writers in difficulties with their plot: 'When in doubt, have a man come through the door with a gun in his hand.'

6 Elmore Leonard, 2002. *Ten Rules of Writing*. Quoted in *The Guardian*, 20 February 2010. (See 'Useful websites' on page 112. Site last retrieved 30 May 2010.)

7 'People make a text real by realizing it as discourse, that is to say by relating it to specific contexts of communal cultural values and attitudes. And this reality does not travel with the text.' H. G. Widdowson, 2003. *Defining Issues in English Language Teaching*. Oxford University Press. p. 98.

8 Kazuo Ishiguro: Author statement on the British Council contemporary writers website. (See 'Useful websites' on page 112. Site last retrieved 29 May 2010.)

9   This comment appears in a collection of comments about Bookworms on the librarything website, a free online book club. (See 'Useful websites' on page 112.) Contributors do not use their real names. Site last retrieved on 27 May 2010.

10 Maryanne Wolf, 2008. *Proust and the Squid: The Story and Science of the Reading Brain*. Icon Books Ltd, Cambridge. p. 224. This is a fascinating account of the development of reading, and how it changes the actual wiring of the brain.

11 Philip Pullman, prize-winning author of the trilogy *His Dark Materials*, writes and speaks with passion of his concern on how reading is dealt with in schools in Britain. This is from the *Isis Lecture* he gave at the 2003 Oxford Literary Festival (available in full in pdf format on the Philip Pullman website. See 'Useful websites' on page 112.)

The danger of tests and league tables and so on is that they demand clear, unequivocal, one-dimensional results. In order to give the sort of result that can be tabulated and measured, they force every kind of response to a piece of writing through a sort of coarse-grained mesh so that it comes out black or white, on or off, yes or no, this or that. In a multiple-choice test there's no provision to say *both*, or *all of them sometimes but mostly this*, or *this today but that yesterday and who knows what tomorrow*, and not at all *something else quite different from any of these*, and certainly not ever *I love this. It made my heart turn over, I was so happy when I read it*.'

12 Daniel Pennac, 2006. Trs. Sarah Adams. *The Rights of the Reader*. Walker Books Ltd, London. pp. 128–9. First published in 1992, this passionate defence of reading for pleasure has sold more than a million copies in France. Worth reading for the Quentin Blake illustrations alone.

13 Philip Pullman. *Isis Lecture*, Oxford Literary Festival, 2003. *The Guardian*, essay, 30 September 2003. Both are available on the Philip Pullman website. (See 'Useful websites' on page 112. Site last retrieved on 28 May 2010.)

Part 2   Extensive Reading: the practice

3 Series editors' view (2)

Bill Bowler and Sue Parminter

One ELT pioneer whom we greatly admire is Dr Michael West (1888–1973), probably best known as the creator of the General Service List (the 2000 most frequent and most useful words for foreign learners of English) in 1953.

West studied English at Oxford University and later taught English, and trained English teachers in India, then under British control. He was deeply interested in assisting a wide range of students (not just the elite) to learn English. Through his classroom research, he identified the importance of **Extensive Reading** (ER) as an effective way of achieving his aim. In the mid-1920s he edited the *New Method Supplementary Graded Readers*, published by Longman. The original series included folk tales and fairy tales at lower levels, and a number of classics, such as Defoe's *Robinson Crusoe*, at higher levels. These were not the first simplified story books for foreign learners of English to be published, but they contained a number of innovative pedagogic features. Namely, they:

- limited the number of vocabulary items permitted at different levels of the series
- indicated new words in bold type on their first appearance in the story text
- recycled words in the story text in a consistent manner.

Originally developed as supplementary readers to accompany a coursebook series, West's **graded readers** later became independently popular in Iran, Kenya, Nigeria, Palestine, Sri Lanka, Uganda, and other countries.

West's systematic approach to grading, highlighting, and vocabulary recycling in supplementary story texts was adopted from 1932 onwards by Harold E. Palmer in his *Reader System* in Japan, and by Lawrence Faucett in his *Rapid Readers*, published by Oxford University Press between 1933 and 1936.

In a number of ways, West could be considered the 'grandfather' of the modern graded reader and, in our view, any series editor of ELT readers working today owes a great debt to this ground-breaking figure in the field.

A graded readers series is a collection of books that have been specially written, or specially simplified, for foreign learners of English to read for enjoyment or for factual information. We believe that graded readers are a useful interim option which can greatly assist students in making the transition from reading short, simplified texts in the classroom, to reading long authentic texts in English (such as short story collections, biographies, history books, or novels) outside the classroom.

 *Getting it right*

Select the right materials

We have known English residents in Spain who attempt to learn to read in Spanish by using simple illustrated children's story books. However, these are not ideal materials to use in such circumstances. From a positive point of view, such stories may not include much text on each page, the language may be relatively simple overall, and the pictures may assist with the understanding of key vocabulary items, but the lexical content and the cognitive level of books like these are certainly not appropriate for teenage or adult students. The texts are too childish, unappealing to learners' interests, and the fantasy or early-childhood-focused vocabulary items in such stories are irrelevant for older age groups.

A graded readers series is clearly the perfect solution to this problem, providing simple, relevant language and supportive illustrations, together with appealing stories.

↓ WHAT ARE HEADWORDS?

The words allowed at each level of a graded reader series without any highlighting, supporting definition, or illustration are called **headwords**. In any graded reader series these progress from a very limited number of words at beginner level, to a larger numbers of words at higher levels. The examples in the table below are taken from the Dominoes graded reader series, which we edit. This series follows the lower levels of The Oxford Bookworms Library grading system:

Level	Number of headwords
Intermediate	1,000
Pre-intermediate	700
Elementary	400
Beginner	250

TABLE 3.1 *A list of headwords from the lower levels of The Oxford Bookworms Library grading system*

A number of additional new words not in the headword lists will always be necessary in order to tell any story smoothly and naturally. In a detective story, for example, the words *crime, criminal, detective, investigate, suspect, innocent,* and *guilty* will probably occur many times. We therefore include words like these in bold text with a simple English definition on their first appearance in the different Dominoes **adaptations** of Conan Doyle's *Sherlock Holmes* stories, for example.

↓ IS WRITING A GRADED READER AN ART OR A SCIENCE?

Writing and editing a graded reader is both an art and a science. The scientific side of our work involves making sure that the story text remains within the following parameters for the level of the book:

- the headwords that are allowed
- the number of 'new' words allowed in addition to the headwords (In Dominoes there are 10–12 new words in each chapter. This is a greater amount of new lexis than permitted in some other graded readers series, but we believe that one of the benefits of ER is that it helps students to acquire vocabulary naturally as they read.)
- the grammatical structures allowed (We cannot expect beginner-level students to read and understand a third conditional sentence, for example!)
- the number of chapters (Dominoes readers progress from six chapters at Starter Level to ten chapters at Level 3.)
- the average number of words in each chapter. (In the Dominoes series, we ensure sufficient room for a considerable amount of illustration to help students' motivation and to support their visual understanding of the verbal text.)

The art of writing or editing a good graded reader story involves all of the above, while at the same time ensuring that the story interests and holds the reader, the characters are vivid, the dialogue is believable, and each chapter ends at an exciting moment in the story, arousing the reader's desire to know what happens next. The test of a well-written graded reader, we believe, is that a native speaker reading it would not necessarily be aware that the vocabulary and grammar in the story are restricted. They would simply enjoy the story.

↓ WHY WE DECIDED TO FOLLOW THE BOOKWORMS GRADING SYSTEM

Looking at some of the very early series of published graded readers, we can see that they were educationally sound, but not always very satisfying to read. The style was often somewhat clumsy. If you study them carefully, you become aware that the writer is avoiding a vocabulary item above the headword level by using a wordy paraphrase. The stories themselves in some of these early generation graded readers are often simplified and shortened to such an extent that the characters become colourless, and the dialogue uninteresting. In certain cases, key elements of the plot are omitted, making the graded story difficult to follow unless the reader is able to refer back to the original, ungraded story to check what happens.

This is what so impressed us about the Bookworms series of graded readers when we first used them in our English language teaching work in the early 1990s. This seemed a new type of graded reader, written in a smooth and natural style, with lively characters, vivid dialogue, and cliff-hanging chapter endings. For us, Bookworms represented a new generation of graded reader where the stories were told or retold freshly for foreign language learners. We were especially impressed by the way Bookworms treated classic stories, which were recreated dramatically within the limitations of each level, rather than being summarized and abridged in a cold and sometimes awkward way, as in earlier readers series. This is why when we began editing the original Dominoes graded readers in 2000, we decided to follow the Bookworms method of storytelling and use the Bookworms grading system.

↓ HOW IMPORTANT IS GOOD STORYTELLING STYLE IN A GRADED READER?

In Dominoes, we have tried to follow the strong storytelling tradition that we first met in this new generation of graded readers. Our aim is to bring well-written and motivating reading material to language learners, using all possible language and artwork resources in order to make the stories lively and motivating for the readers.

In the case of adaptations of famous stories, it is very important to remain true to the spirit of the original. There may, however, be cultural references that need explaining in order to make a past classic understandable for today's readers. Times change, and a graded reader retelling must take account of that fact. Here are a couple of examples:

First, to take Charles Dickens – his novels originally came out in serialized form in newspapers and he was paid by the word. Long, descriptive passages and a huge cast of characters were suitable for the context of his time. But these days all of us (especially teenagers) have a shorter attention span, perhaps because we are strongly influenced by the immediacy of movies and television. When we read for pleasure, even in our mother tongue, we want to get straight to the action. We are generally not interested in having to read long, detailed descriptions of different London streets and the people in them before we are introduced to the main characters and the key action of the story. This is especially true when someone is reading in a foreign language. The art of retelling a story like *Nicholas Nickleby* or *Hard Times* as a graded reader is to keep something of the flavour of Dickens without boring the students and making them want to give up. With stories like *The Last of the Mohicans* (a classic of American literature, but rather challenging to read in the original, even for a native speaker), series editors can often feel they are rescuing a wonderful story that might not otherwise be read. In some ways it is a little like remaking a slow-moving, silent black-and-white classic movie for today's audiences and producing it in full-colour, with contemporary actors and a modern music soundtrack!

Second, a humorous or a poetic style is often the most difficult to recreate in a graded language version. But to be faithful to the original, this has to be attempted. We have always tried to ensure that at least some of the original authors' humorous style remains in the Dominoes retellings of stories such as Wilde's *Lord Arthur Savile's Crime* or Jerome K. Jerome's *The Faithful Ghost*; similarly, we made great efforts to ensure that the descriptions of Corfu, for example, in *My Family and Other Animals* capture at least something of Durrell's original poetic use of language.

There is something very elegant about the extreme simplicity of style forced upon a writer or adapter working at starter level, and using only narrative present tenses to write or retell a story. Yet Dominoes stories like Shakespeare's *The Tempest*, or Wilde's *The Happy Prince*, show what can be achieved, even at such low levels.

↓ WHAT DOES A SERIES EDITOR DO?

An important part of our job involves selecting stories to be developed as Dominoes readers. As the series grows, we try to make sure that we keep a balance between our six genre categories:

- television and film adventures (often preferred by teenage boys)
- world literature (not just English or American stories)
- mystery and horror (popular with both teenage boys and girls)
- human interest (often preferred by teenage girls)
- story collections (good for readers who are looking for a number of short, free-standing stories)
- true tales (a welcome alternative to fiction).

Another of our functions is to work closely with authors who are writing Dominoes readers. In addition to detailed story editing, we also:

- give suggestions on plot development, characterization, historic or geographic setting, and exciting endings for chapters
  (We have particularly enjoyed working in these areas with Joyce Hannam, author of *The Curse of the Mummy*, *Ariadne's Story*, and *The Vesuvius Mosaic* – all graded reader 'historical novels' which blend fact and fiction in an interesting way.)
- give suggestions to authors writing adaptations of story collections, on which stories would be appropriate for a thematic collection
- advise authors working on adaptations of well-known stories, on which parts of an original text to miss out, summarize briefly, or focus on, in order to fit the story into the agreed page plan
- try to make sure that all story texts read smoothly and dramatically
- check that all the graded readers in the Dominoes series meet the agreed grading guidelines in terms of headwords and grammatical structures for different levels, and the number of glossed words that can be introduced.

Aside from this, we edit the exercises on the 'Before Reading' and between-chapter activity pages, and make sure they work well to support the students' reading experience by:

- encouraging students to predict story content before they start to read
- checking and **scaffolding** students' understanding of the story as it unfolds
- offering students a chance to activate **recognition vocabulary** that they have met in the story context
- encouraging while-reading prediction of what will happen next.

As the Dominoes series editors, it is also our responsibility to check that:

- different types of post-reading projects (imaginative, creative, Internet research based, or language based) are included in each reader, and to ensure that a variety of projects is offered across each level and across the series as a whole
- projects are staged step by step, and doable by students at that level
- relevant grammar points are included on the grammar pages in each reader to suit the level and the particular story
- explanations in the Grammar Check boxes on the grammar pages are easy to understand, and that they give students sufficient guidance for them to complete the practice exercises that follow
- story, activity page, and project artwork is clear and helpful and, in the case of historical stories, as accurate as possible
- MultiROM exercise and game content is appropriate and suitably organized, and that MultiROM exercises are pedagogically sound.

↓ HOW CAN WE SUPPORT EXTENSIVE READING?

There are a number of ways in which we can support students in their ER. These include:

- giving teacher-led support in the classroom (by pre-teaching vocabulary, asking students questions about the story, and how they are managing their reading, etc.)
- providing an audio version of the story text (ideally a dramatized version, with music and sound effects, and different actors' voices) for students to listen to as they read
- offering students photocopiable task sheets of different kinds
- using a digital learning management system
- providing students with 'in-book' tasks to complete before, during, or after they read.

 **Getting it right**

Structure and support your students' ER

We are particularly interested in guiding Extensive Reading to make it more manageable for all students, and not just something for highly competent readers to undertake. There is a lot you, the teacher, can do in class to help organize students' reading out of class. Nevertheless, 'in-book' activities can be very useful to help you structure and support the students' experience of ER. This is especially true if you are dealing with students new to ER (and therefore less confident).

Our interest in the usefulness of 'in-book' support grew out of our experiences in Alicante with Spanish students trying to cope with unsupported graded reading in English. As a result of some of these students' negative experiences with ER, we became increasingly interested in offering a more structured approach by including prediction, comprehension, and vocabulary tasks as integral parts of the graded reader story. Dominoes-style pre-reading and post-reading activities offer the sort of 'good practice' techniques which an experienced teacher might employ naturally, namely:

Try this ☞ **Chunk reading text**

Break down a longer reading text into shorter 'chunks' to make it more manageable for students. You can also build students' critical reading skill abilities, through tasks focused on predicting, hypothesizing, inferring, summarizing, comparing, deducing, transferring information, putting themselves in someone else's shoes, visualizing, evaluating, and so on.

Some people may assume that, because Dominoes graded readers include support tasks between story chapters, they are somehow not designed for ER, but are only intended for **Intensive Reading** (IR) in the classroom. However, this was certainly not our aim when we began editing Dominoes. Although short extracts taken from a Dominoes graded reader story *can* be used for IR skills work in the classroom (perhaps to awaken students' interest in borrowing the book from the readers library to read extensively later), our underlying intention is simply to provide a familiar and supportive framework within which ER can take place. In our view this reading can be done in class, in a library or self-access centre, at home during evening and weekends, or in the school holidays. We believe that if teachers offer ER materials at a realistically achievable level and include sufficient 'in-book' support for the task, ER will become more manageable and will therefore be done.

How can we check that students are reading outside class?

Another of our aims in Dominoes has been to provide teachers with an easy way to check that outside class reading is actually being done. There are a number of different 'outside-the-reader' materials and activities that can provide ER support and accountability and can also help to motivate students (especially teenagers) to read extensively.

Accountability tools (which help you to check that the reading has been done) include:

Try this ☞ **Devise accountability activities**

- activity pages to be completed by students after they have read each chapter
- an easily marked end-of-book pen-and-paper quiz (a multiple-choice test is ideal for this, because it is easy to administer and quick to mark)
- project work, to be kept in a student's 'Reading Portfolio' (a folder which includes the student's ER-related work to be assessed, possibly instead of formal assessment).

In our experience, students dislike formal written ER testing, and being asked to complete the same task (such as 'write a summary') after every graded reader they finish. From these observations, we draw the conclusion that it is preferable for teachers to offer students other options.

Try this ☞ **Create assessment options**

- post-reading tests, or quizzes, which are relatively short and easy to complete ('tick the box', rather than 'write a paragraph'. Such evaluation tools could even be computerized if digital testing is an available option.)
- different post-reading projects, to provide variety and choice
- a written model text for students to follow, together with supportive scaffolding in the form of a sequence of staged writing activities from controlled, to less controlled, to freer and more personalized.

How can we support writing and speaking tasks coming out of Extensive Reading?

One of the factors that may cause problems for students in reading-related written or discussion work is the lack of adequate preparation time. As a result of limited class time, teachers may find themselves asking students to have ideas, and simultaneously to express them in correct English. It is not surprising in such circumstances that reading-related discussion work often fails, or that reading-related written work may seem boring. There are, however, ways of providing students with genuine opportunities to communicate their thoughts, observations, and feelings.

Try this ☞ **Do reading circle discussion work**

One way of supporting reading-related discussion work is to put students into **reading circles** (or reading teams) and to assign each individual student within a team a specific role. (This technique is dealt with more fully in Mark Furr's chapter on Reading Circles. See page 63.)

Try this ☞ **Provide graphic organizer task sheets**

Another way of helping students to organize their thoughts prior to a reading-related discussion or writing activity, is to provide them with a **graphic organizer** task sheet on which to make notes. An example of a graphic organizer page is given on page 42.

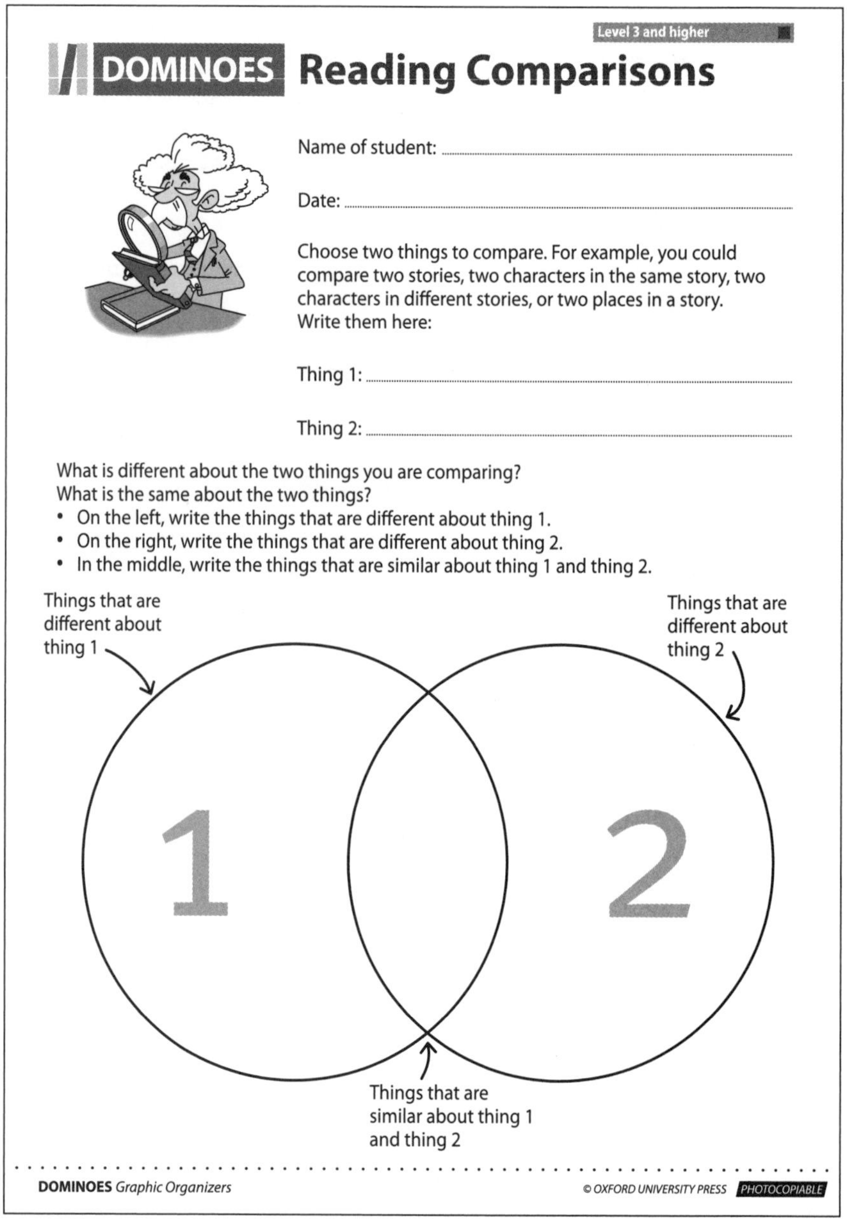

Level 3 and higher

DOMINOES **Reading Comparisons**

Name of student: ....

Date: ....

Choose two things to compare. For example, you could compare two stories, two characters in the same story, two characters in different stories, or two places in a story.
Write them here:

Thing 1: ....

Thing 2: ....

What is different about the two things you are comparing?
What is the same about the two things?

- On the left, write the things that are different about thing 1.
- On the right, write the things that are different about thing 2.
- In the middle, write the things that are similar about thing 1 and thing 2.

DOMINOES *Graphic Organizers* © OXFORD UNIVERSITY PRESS PHOTOCOPIABLE

FIGURE 3.1 *A graphic organizer page focusing on comparing two characters*

Graphic organizers are relatively common in literacy and language study materials published in North America, but (in our experience) not so frequent in British-produced EFL materials. The organizers provide an excellent supportive framework for students to be able to organize their reading work and note down their ideas before reading, after reading, and in preparation for reading-related speaking or writing tasks.

Why this works

Choosing from the variety of options outlined in this chapter increases students' motivation to read extensively because they:

- are offered reading material of interest to them, in manageable chunks and at a suitable level
- feel reassured by the doable, **process-based** approach to reading accountability
- feel supported by the scaffolding of materials and classroom interactions available to them
- are aware that they have a variety of choices in terms of post-reading assessment activities.

4 Class readers

Sue Parminter and Bill Bowler

Using a **class reader** means that all the students in a class are working on the same **graded reader** at the same time. You, as the teacher, might perhaps set a number of readers over an academic year, each reader to be covered over a number of weeks.

Advantages of using a class reader

The main reason why you might opt to use a class reader, at least in the initial stages of **Extensive Reading** (ER) work, is the fact that you have control over the reading process, and can easily check that students are in fact doing the reading. This approach may be particularly appropriate for weaker, less confident students, who are not yet used to or very well equipped for independent, self-directed reading. Using a class reader can be a good way of training a class of students in ER skills such as ignoring unknown words, guessing vocabulary from context, ongoing prediction, and focusing on the key content of the story.

Other related advantages of using class readers are that you can set the same homework for all the students who are working on the same book, and apply the same exit test once they have all finished reading the book. Evaluation of students' reading is thus reliable, since all students are being evaluated on their ability to cope with the same reading material.

A shared alternative reality

Another real advantage of using class readers is that they provide a rich 'alternative reality' which the whole class shares. When students in a class know each other well, talking about their daily lives in English can seem rather artificial and boring, since students probably know all the answers to any questions they may ask their classmates already, through previous conversations together in their mother tongue. But when students are talking about the characters or events in a story and discussing their feelings and observations, this is new information. Consequently the information gap that needs to be bridged in English is an authentic one. In addition, all the students in the class will know everything there is to know about the story, the vocabulary, and the structures that are used to tell it. They are thus both linguistically and factually well equipped to do the reading-related activities you set them.

Choosing a class reader

If you decide to use class readers, you will obviously choose one that you hope will appeal to all the students in your class. This is a particular challenge with teenage classes, since gender differences influence reading preferences quite strongly during the adolescent years.

Some classic stories, such as Dumas' *The Three Musketeers* and *The Count of Monte Cristo* are suitable choices in this respect, since they contain adventure as well as human interest elements and are therefore likely to satisfy students of both genders.

When selecting original graded stories, it is a good idea to read the catalogue description and the back-cover blurb (which often summarize the story in a tantalizing way), in order to find out whether the characters and situations in the story are likely to appeal to the majority of the students in your class. Of course your choice can never please all the students all the time! However, if over the course of several months you select class readers from a variety of different story types (crime, thriller, mystery, human interest, adventure, fantasy, horror, true story, etc.), all the different students' reading tastes are likely to be catered for at different times during the academic year.

Try this  **Mix and match**

It is a good idea to ensure that you choose a mixture of classic stories, some of which may be familiar to students already through film and TV **adaptations**, and are therefore not so daunting to read in English.

Try this  **Keep them guessing**

Select some original graded reader stories, or adaptations of less familiar stories, where the students do not know in advance anything of the story content. They will be naturally curious to see how the story develops and ends.

Choosing the right level

There are different criteria for choosing the correct level for the class reader. Two of the most common are listed below.

✓ *Getting it right*

Select an appropriate level

1 Select a reader pitched at the students' active structural level (for example, if students have just studied the past simple, select a reader using past pimple and narrative present tenses, but not present perfect).
2 Select a reader pitched slightly below the students' active structural level (for example, if students have just studied the past simple, select a reader using narrative present tenses, but not past simple).

The first option is probably the most frequent, but there is a lot to be said for choosing a reader which will be relatively easy for students to read, since this can help create the positive feeling of reading for pleasure in English that readers will experience when reading for pleasure in their mother tongue. Students may be able to read two lower-pitched class

Class readers

readers enjoyably in the same time that it would take them to read one higher-pitched class reader with some difficulty. Very often publishers will make recommendations of appropriately levelled readers which are suitable to use alongside their different coursebooks, and these can be useful for you to consult as a guide:

Project (3ʳᵈ Edition) Level 1 recommended reading

LESSON THEMES

After units 1–2
Personal information
Family and friends

After units 3–4
My world
Routines

After units 5–6
Places
People

Mulan

The Big Story

Changing Places

Around the World in Eighty Days

The Happy Prince

Starter

Retold by Janet Hardy-Gould

Starter

John Escott

Starter

Alan Hines

Starter

Jules Verne
Text adaptation by Bill Bowler

Starter

Oscar Wilde
Text adaptation by Bill Bowler

When the Emperor calls every man to join the army and fight the enemy, Mulan's father is old and ill, and cannot go. Wearing men's clothes and riding a horse, Mulan leaves her family and fights bravely for the Emperor in her father's place.

She is soon a hero for all the soldiers in the Chinese army. One of them, Ye Ming, is her best friend. But does he know that she is a woman? And can Mulan fall in love with a friend?

'Bring me something new and exciting. Bring me a BIG story!' says Rosie's editor at *The Record* newspaper.

And, when she leaves the office, Rosie does find a story. A story that is bigger than she expects. A story that takes her across Europe, into a dangerous world of art and art thieves.

* *This story is recorded in British English, with some American characters.*

Hal works at the zoo every day and his life isn't exciting – until he meets Tim.

Tim is a movie star. He has a difficult life, and he is unhappy – until he meets Hal.

But when they meet, and agree to change places, interesting things start to happen. And, by changing places, the two men learn what is truly important in their lives.

'Today you can go round the world in eighty days,' says Phileas Fogg. 'Do it, and I pay you £20,000,' says his friend Stuart.

This is the beginning of one of Jules Verne's most exciting stories. Phileas Fogg must get back to London by December 21st or lose all his money. With the help of his servant, Passepartout, Fogg travels in many ways – from train to elephant – and he has some surprising adventures on the way.

The Happy Prince is a beautiful golden statue high up on a column in the city. Everyone loves him.

He feels sad about the city's poor people, but what can he do? He can't leave his column. Then the swallow arrives, and helps the Happy Prince to do many good things.

But what about the swallow's dream of flying to Egypt? And what does the Mayor do when the Happy Prince loses all his gold?

Starter syllabus A1 Average word count 2,250 250 Headwords
Grammar: present simple, present continuous, modals *can, must*

DOMINOES

| Book 978 0 19 4247061 | Book 978 0 19 424710 8 | Book 978 0 19 424708 5 | Book 978 0 19 424701 6 | Book 978 0 19 424712 2 |
| MultiROM Pack 978 0 19 424670 5 AmE | MultiROM Pack 978 0 19 424674 3 BrE * | MultiROM Pack 978 0 19 424672 9 AmE | MultiROM Pack 978 0 19 424665 1 BrE | MultiROM Pack 978 0 19 424676 7 BrE |

🎧 AUDIO CD AVAILABLE

PHOTOCOPIABLE © OXFORD UNIVERSITY PRESS 2010

FIGURE 4.1   *Correlation of graded reader level to coursebook level*

Mixed ability classes and class readers

In mixed ability classes, where stronger and weaker students are working together on the same class reader, stronger students may finish activities earlier than their classmates. Quick students can often feel frustrated at having to wait until the slower members of the class have caught up with them.

✓ *Getting it right*

Provide tasks for mixed-ability classes

One solution to this problem of mixed ability classes is to provide 'early finishers' with extra tasks to occupy them until the whole class has finished the main task, and you and the class are ready to move on. The ideal type of task for this purpose is one which requires no preparation from you, and only basic classroom resources. Here are some suggestions:

Try this 👉 **Get students to prepare a puzzle**

The students prepare a crossword puzzle, or a 'word-bit' puzzle, using new words from the reader.

● wild	● cies	● pesti	● in
● sect	● life	● rain	● cyc
● cide	● nuc	● spe	● radio
● lear	● lone	● active	● forest

FIGURE 4.2 *A 'word-bit' puzzle using new vocabulary from* Green Planet *(Dominoes level 2)*

Answer key

wild/life in/sect pesti/cide nuc/lear spe/cies cyc/lone rain/forest radio/active

Try this 👉 **Ask students to prepare letter clue sentences**

The students prepare initial letter clue sentences such as those below, using new words from the reader.

> 1 C_____ is a hard, black thing from the ground that we burn to give heat. (coal)
> 2 O_____ is a thick liquid from under the ground that we use for energy. (oil)
> 3 The a_____ is the mixture of gases around the Earth. (atmosphere)
> 4 Coal and diamonds are made of c_____ , and it is in all living things. (carbon)
> 5 O_____ is a gas in the air that people and animals need to live. (oxygen)
> 6 To m_____ is to become liquid after becoming warmer. (melt)

FIGURE 4.3 *Initial letter clue sentences using new vocabulary from* Climate Change *(Bookworms level 2)*

Class readers

Try this  **Invite students to prepare a letter square**

The students prepare a letter square puzzle using new words from the reader.

I	W	P	E	N	A	L	T	Y	D
T	H	R	O	W	H	E	N	G	A
K	I	C	K	L	E	A	G	U	E
Z	S	J	X	H	S	H	O	O	T
O	T	S	S	M	A	T	C	H	Z
J	L	F	H	N	X	K	C	M	W
D	E	F	E	N	D	O	K	U	R
A	J	R	A	I	C	L	U	B	U
Y	T	S	D	S	C	O	R	E	L
C	O	R	N	E	R	F	Y	R	E

FIGURE 4.4   *A letter square puzzle using new vocabulary from* The Beautiful Game (Bookworms level 2)

Answer key
(Across) PENALTY THROW KICK LEAGUE SHOOT MATCH DEFEND CLUB SCORE CORNER
(Down) WHISTLE HEAD RULE

✓ *Getting it right*   **Encourage pairwork cooperation**

An alternative solution to the problem of mixed-ability classes is to avoid having 'early finishers' altogether by grouping students in strong–weak pairs for reading-related activities to help weaker students to keep up.

↓ BUILDING MOTIVATION BEFORE READING

With a class reader approach, students have no choice as to which story to read. Therefore it is vital for you to build up individual students' motivation and interest in the story before the class starts to read the book you have selected for them. Here are various techniques you can use as 'whole class' motivation-builders:

Try this ☞ **Generate interest through pictures**

Use the cover illustration of your chosen class reader to generate interest in the story. An example of this type of activity is given below.

Look at the cover picture and answer these questions:
- Are these people rich or poor, do you think?
- What is the relationship between the boy and the old man?
- Is the boy afraid of the big dog, do you think?
- Is the old man healthy, do you think?
- Is the old man happy, do you think?
- What does the boy think of the old man?
- What does the old man think of the boy?

FIGURE 4.5   *A cover picture prediction activity for* Little Lord Fauntleroy (Bookworms level 1)

Try this ☞ **Offer a variety of other options**

- Ask the students to read the back-cover blurb or a short summary of the beginning of the story and use the information to predict what will happen in the story.
- Give the students the chapter titles and ask them to predict from them what will happen in the story.
- Ask students to listen to the opening of the story on an audio CD and to predict what will happen next.
- Show a scene from the start of a commercially produced DVD of a classic story in order to introduce the main characters and the start of the plot. Then ask students to predict what will happen in the story.
  (NOTE: It is important to check on copyright restrictions before using a DVD in this way.)
- Prepare a 'word rose' featuring key vocabulary from the story and ask students to predict the story content. This also allows you to pre-teach any unknown vocabulary. (We are indebted to Mario Rinvolucri for the idea of the Word Rose.)

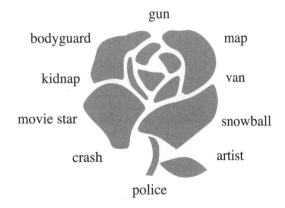

FIGURE 4.6   *A 'word rose' prediction activity for* Kidnap! *(Dominoes Starter level)*

When the whole class is reading the same book, it can be a good idea to let the students listen to an audio recording of the class reader (if available) as they follow the text in their books. The benefits of this approach are:

- Audio recordings made by native speaker actors provide good pronunciation models for students, especially for names of characters and places in a story, which students cannot look up in a dictionary.
- Students who may not understand the phrasing and meaning of sentences when they see them on the page can be supported by listening to the story read aloud, since a storyteller's stresses, pauses, and intonation patterns help to reinforce and clarify the meaning of the written words.
- Weaker students, who may become 'blocked' and stop reading when they meet words they do not understand will be encouraged to ignore unknown words and to move on through the story text as they listen to the audio recording.
- Audio recordings can help to bring the story alive for students who are not strongly motivated by silent reading.

While-reading activities

While students are reading a chapter of a class reader, it can be useful to give them some comprehension tasks to check and support their understanding of the story. Below are a few classic 'while-reading' tasks.

Try this ☞ **Create task sheets**

1 Write some sentences about the story for the students to mark T (true) or F (false).
2 Write some questions about the story, with multiple choice answers for the students to select.
3 Provide a jumbled list of story events for the students to sequence in the correct order.
4 Write and distribute a short summary of the story with some factual mistakes in it for students to correct.
5 Prepare some split sentences about the story for students to match up correctly.
6 Give each student a summary of the story with gaps in it to complete.

Written tasks like these can be completed in pairs or individually. However, even with individual work, it is a good idea to include a pairwork comparison mini-stage before conducting whole-class feedback. This gives weaker students a chance to check their ideas with those of stronger classmates and to get ideas on task items which they cannot complete easily on their own.

Try this ☞ **Organize team games**

When students have finished reading a chapter of their class reader, you could divide the class into two teams, each with a different team name ('Booksellers' and 'Librarians', for example). Each team then prepares a number of questions based on the chapter they have just read for the other team to answer. When the students' questions are ready, you organize a class quiz, awarding a point to each team for every question they answer correctly.

Try this ☞ **Show MultiROM activities**

When a class reader is accompanied by a MultiROM, you could show some of the MultiROM activities on an interactive whiteboard (or on a classroom wall, using a data show projector). These activities can also be turned into team competitions.

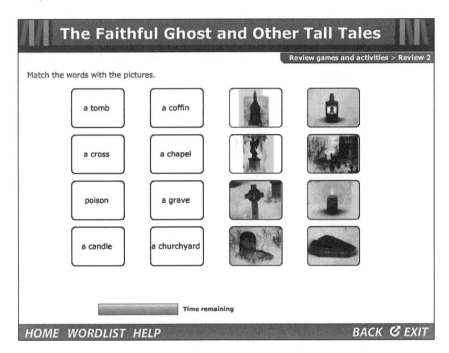

FIGURE 4.7   *An interactive MultiROM activity from* The Faithful Ghost *(Dominoes level 3)*

↓ WHERE IS THE READING ACTUALLY DONE?

It is important to stress that, even with a class reader approach, not all the actual reading needs to be done in the classroom. Of course it is necessary to demonstrate techniques such as reading while listening to the audio CD in class time. However, we would advise against asking students to read the text of a class reader aloud, sentence by sentence around the class. This kind of **lockstep** reading approach can be extremely boring and slow for faster readers, and highly embarrassing for students whose pronunciation of English is weak.

Try this ☞ **Organize preparatory work and check activities**

When you have only a limited amount of time to deal with class reader work in the classroom, set students some preparatory reading homework to do outside class. Then, for the next class reader lesson, you could organize some comprehension check activities to ensure that the outside class reading has actually been done.

Vocabulary records

Working with a class reader can provide a useful springboard into vocabulary work for the whole class. Ask each student to keep a personalized vocabulary notebook containing all the new words they meet in the course of their reading. Often the new lexis will be picked out in bold in the story text and glossed on the page (as in Dominoes), or listed and defined at the back of the class reader (as in the Oxford Bookworms Library). However, since different students in a class will have varying degrees of vocabulary proficiency, it is important not to limit individual vocabulary records to such highlighted items. Encourage your students to include in their notebook *all* unfamiliar vocabulary items in the story. It is a good idea for students to include the following details for each vocabulary item that they record:

- the new word itself
- a pronunciation guide of some kind (showing word stress, silent letters, and perhaps also phonetics)
- a definition of the word in simple English (or a small picture, where appropriate)
- an example sentence to show how the word works in context (this could be drawn from the class reader itself, or a memorable personalized example created by the student)
- a note of the page and the line in the class reader where the new word first appears
- a translation into the student's mother tongue.

After-reading activities

Once students have finished a class reader, set the class some follow-up writing or discussion activities of different kinds to give students a chance to respond personally, imaginatively, or creatively to what they have read, to consolidate their reading, and to round off work on one class reader before they move on to read another.

Try this ☞ **Encourage students to write questions**

Ask your students to write some post-reading questions on the story to ask each other. The questions can be either yes/no or open-ended in style. Below is an example of an open-ended post-reading activity:

> Which of the characters in these stories would you like to …
>
> 1 give some advice to?
> 2 invite to a party?
> 3 take home to meet your parents?
> 4 sit next to on a long flight?
> 5 never meet at all?

FIGURE 4.8 *Post-reading activity from* Doors to a Wider Place: Stories from Australia *(Bookworms level 4)*

Using graphic organizers

In order to give students a chance to organize their thoughts before they write, take part in a discussion activity, or make an oral presentation, you may wish to give them the opportunity to make notes on a graphic organizer page. Graphic organizers are highly visual and memorable ways of encouraging learners to brainstorm and arrange their ideas before they format them in a written text, or in spoken form.

Below are two examples of graphic organizers. The first, from Dominoes, can help students to compare any two class readers of their choice.

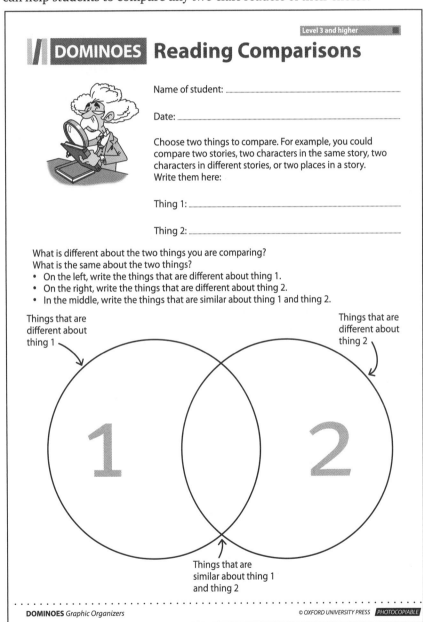

FIGURE 4.9   *Graphic organizer for reading comparisons from Dominoes*

The second example, from the Bookworms Club Plot Pyramid page, can help students to analyse the development of a story plot.

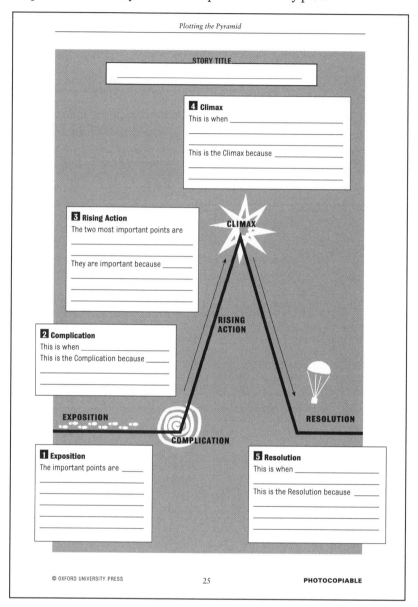

FIGURE 4.10 *Plot pyramid from Bookworms Club*

Ensuring variety in post-reading activities

 **Getting it right**

Suggest a variety of activities

If you always ask students to produce a written essay, or to take part in a teacher-led discussion on the class reader they have just read, this can become predictable and demotivating. Try to suggest different kinds of post-reading activities to keep students motivated. There are many possible and interesting alternative activities.

Try this ☞ **Suggest multi-media activities**
1 Ask the students to make a poster which combines written text and illustration.
2 Get the students to prepare and deliver an oral PowerPoint™ presentation.
3 Ask the students to perform a role-play as characters from the story.
4 Ask the students to put their written work up on a class notice board for other students to read.
5 Encourage the students to write a dramatized scene based on the class reader story, then to act it out and make an audio or video recording of it.
6 Suggest that the students keep an individual reading portfolio where they file copies of their post-reading tasks, either as work in progress or as finished work for display.

↓ EVALUATING READING

When all your students are working with the same class reader, it is extremely easy to set the same written test for everyone. For teachers concerned with issues of test security, it is worth considering the preparation of an A version and a B version of the test. With a multiple choice test this is relatively easy to do, simply by changing the order of test items and preparing an A marking key and a B marking key to match the different versions of the test paper.

To be fair to students who suffer from exam nerves, it is a good idea to include the following evaluation categories in the overall assessment of individual students' skills in ER, giving them an overall mark that reflects:

- the students' achievement in any reading-related writing tasks they do throughout the year
- the students' achievement in any reading-related speaking tasks they do throughout the year
- the students' achievement in the formal written test.

Why this works

Selecting from the different options summarized in this chapter increases students' motivation to work on a class reader because they:

- feel supported in their reading by your classroom staging of pre-reading activities, your custom-designed 'while-reading' task sheets, and the variety of post-reading tasks you offer them
- feel supported in their reading by their classmates and recognize that shared work on a reader goes beyond solitary reading, taking them into stimulating areas such as listening and discussion work, personalized vocabulary recording and note-taking, peer teaching, film studies, art, IT, drama, and presentation skills
- feel reassured by your **process-based approach** to the evaluation of reading throughout the year.

5 Libraries

Nick Bullard

↓ WHY USE A LIBRARY?

A library of **graded readers** is one of the better ways of making **Extensive Reading** (ER) available to students. It gives students access to a range of reading materials and provides ways of encouraging and monitoring their reading. By using a library rather than teacher-selected materials, it becomes possible for students to have a much wider access to reading material. It also allows students to read at the level which is most comfortable for them.

↓ CLASS LIBRARIES OR INSTITUTION LIBRARIES?

Not all institutions have libraries. Where there is a library, it may well be an appropriate place to house a collection of graded readers. The librarian(s) will then take responsibility for loans and returns, and students will develop the habit of using the library. However, not all institutions can offer an easily accessible library (it may be in a different building), and not all librarians are prepared to cooperate in allowing graded readers into a library. The alternative is to develop a class library of readers that can be based in or near the actual classroom. This gives the students easier access, but requires you, the teacher, to be more involved in library organization. This is not usually too time-consuming, and much of the administration can often be delegated to students.

↓ WHAT A LIBRARY DOES FOR YOUR STUDENTS

ER is one of the most effective ways of increasing a student's contact with English. In a typical secondary school environment, students may spend perhaps two to four hours a week in an English class, and perhaps an hour or two more on homework. This is simply not enough contact to ensure a sound working knowledge of the language. Simply reading, using **graded materials**, is a very effective way of increasing contact with the language. Additionally, because students are reading for a purpose (to get at the story) motivation can be very high.

Students will be even more motivated if they have the autonomy that a library can provide. In a library, they can choose their topic and level. They can read one book a week if they wish. They also have the choice *not* to read a book that they don't like, or find too difficult.

Because reading, and particularly reading by choosing a book from a library, is fully under the students' control, it increases their autonomy. Not only can the students choose what they want to read, they can also choose when and where they will read. They can stop reading when they like and resume when they like. They can go back and read a sentence or a chapter again, if they so wish. Developing learner autonomy is one of the key objectives in education, and a library of graded readers is an excellent way of doing this.

Most importantly, a library gives students far greater access to reading material. As Richard Day points out in Chapter 1, the greater the quantity of reading a student does, the greater the benefit of an Extensive Reading Programme (ERP). A library with just 50–100 books gives each student the possibility of reading *all* the books. This is a far greater exposure to reading than can be achieved in any other way. Many library programmes report average students reading between five and ten books a year, with exceptional students reading in excess of 50. The increased contact with English that reading on this scale can give to students is remarkable. Some of the benefits are developed in Minas Mahmood's Chapter 8 (see page 90). The benefits that a student can derive from this quantity of reading can hardly be exaggerated.

 *Getting it right*

> **Brief colleagues and parents**
>
> In some circumstances it may be necessary to brief colleagues and parents about the objectives of the library. The educational benefits of an ERP are not necessarily transparent and obvious to all, and they may need some explanation.

↓ CONSTRUCTING A LIBRARY

Number of readers

For a class readers library, it is best to aim for more books than there are students in the class. For a class of 30 students, 50 books is the desirable minimum number of readers, so that there is enough choice left for students wanting to take out another book.

If the class covers a wide range of student ability it will be necessary to expand the library to allow sufficient choice at any particular level.

Selection of readers

As students begin to read extensively it is very important that the library has a good range of readers at a low level. For students to benefit from their reading, they need to be reading fluently and without recourse to a dictionary. The students should be reading in order to follow the story, and while the occasional unknown word will not be a distraction, if the number of unknown words rises above one or two per cent, the story will be lost.

Libraries

Similarly, if students are confronted with grammar which is far beyond their experience, their reading will falter. In addition, many students will be unfamiliar with reading extensively even in their own language, so it is important to minimize the obstacles for them.

Most graded reader series offer a full range of levels and, unless students are well above Intermediate level, some titles from the lowest levels should be included. If the series includes The Oxford Bookworms Library or Dominoes, the Starter level is ideal for this. It is better for students to start at a level below their own and then move up through the levels than for them to start at too high a level and get frustrated. Reading at below their level is nevertheless beneficial for students. It shows them that reading is a way of conveying meaning, as well as providing enjoyment. It contextualizes the language they have learned in class, develops their reading fluency, and demonstrates that reading is not necessarily an overly challenging activity. It also extends their contact with the language beyond the classroom.

In at least two of the programmes described in the case studies later in this book, it was found essential to include readers at Starter level – and these were enjoyed by students of all abilities.

 *Getting it right*

Help your students to choose their own level

Nevertheless, students may want to identify the level that corresponds to their own 'comfort zone'. The Oxford Bookworms Library provides a series of online level tests for students. (See 'Useful websites' on page 112.) These can help students to choose a level to start on.

Note that there may be pressure from colleagues, administrators, parents, and even the students themselves to push towards too high a level at first. This needs to be tactfully resisted. The role of an ER library is to provide materials that can be read fluently.

For an ERP to be successful, the reading materials available must respond not only to a variety of levels but to a variety of tastes. Some students will only be interested in true stories, so there will need to be a selection of these. Other students may have tastes as diverse as science fiction or crime. The advantage of a library is that it can provide a range of different genres, without imposing a particular genre on a student who is not interested. In selecting readers, a range of levels and genre is essential. Ten titles at each level would be a good starting point, although it may be necessary to add more at some stage.

The cost of the 50–100 readers needed to make up a classroom library is small compared to the benefits the students derive from it. A library of graded readers lasts several years, and the experience of most teachers is that only a small proportion need to be replaced every year through loss or damage.

Often audio recordings of readers are available on CD and these too may be motivating for students. However, audio is by no means essential. If there is a limited budget it may be better to focus on additional books rather than on CDs.

In some contexts, especially with younger learners, there may be cultural or religious concerns about some books. You may need to get the books approved by a Ministry of Education or other body. (See Chapters 7 and 8 for examples that illustrate where this was done successfully.)

↓ LIBRARY ORGANIZATION

If the readers can be integrated into a school library, the organizational requirements are minimal. It will, however, be necessary to encourage students to use the library. It may be useful to set up a series of library visits in the first weeks to develop the habit.

If the readers are kept in the classroom, there is the advantage that the books are easily accessible, but a certain amount of tracking and monitoring is necessary. In many projects, students have shown that they are fully capable of managing this themselves. A key item here is the student's individual record card (see Figure 5.1) which you can also download from the Internet. (See 'Useful websites' on page 112.)

READING DIARY

Name: _____ Class: _____

BOOK TITLE	STAGE	NUMBER OF PAGES/ WORDS	START DATE	FINISH DATE	HOURS SPENT READING	LEVEL			RATING			COMMENTS
						TOO EASY	RIGHT LEVEL	TOO DIFFICULT	☺	😐	☹	

OXFORD **BOOKWORMS**

PHOTOCOPIABLE © OXFORD UNIVERSITY PRESS

FIGURE 5.1   *A student's reading diary*

Libraries

The easiest way to manage this is to provide a record sheet for each student. These sheets should be kept in a folder with the books and completed by the students themselves. It may be complemented with a similar record card inside the front cover of each book, to track the borrowings.

In addition to tracking which student has read which book, a student record sheet also enables the students to record their impressions of the book. Students can be very motivated by being given the opportunity to express their opinion. Furthermore, the opinions of their friends may also be of interest to them when selecting a book.

If students choose a book they don't like, or that they find too difficult, they can simply change it. They don't have to finish every book they choose (although ideally they should finish some!). If students choose a book that is below their level but that they are enjoying nonetheless, that doesn't matter either. There will always be benefits from reading in English at any level.

It may be helpful to set reading targets for students. As noted earlier, many students will read five or ten books a year and a few will read up to 50. Suggesting a target number of books will give students a useful measure to go by. Some teachers prefer to specify a certain number of words, and for this reason many readers series give a word count for each story. The number of words in a reader varies enormously according to level, but averages at around 10,000 words. Over a two or three year period a student might aim for a million words – an impressive and quite attainable figure.

Following up on reading

Simply reading, expressing an opinion, and moving on to another book may be all that students need to keep them reading and benefiting from the ERP. But whatever approach students take, it may also be necessary to introduce more formal after-reading activities. A number of informal activities used for class readers are described in Chapter 6, and some of these are also appropriate for libraries.

However, a more formal series of activities during or after reading may help students to motivate themselves.

Try this ☞ **Explore formal reading activities**

1 Writing a book report can be a valuable after-reading activity, although it is important that it should not interfere with the pleasure of the reading. For this reason it is probably better to keep it short. You may prefer your students to write their book report in their mother tongue so that the task doesn't take too long. Some teachers prefer their students to use English.

2 Tests can be a more straightforward way of following up on reading, and Thomas Robb (see Chapter 10) provides an elegant approach to this. The advantage of this solution is that it doesn't take up too much of your or your students' time. It is important for students to spend their time reading rather than doing tests or writing reports.

Tests for both Bookworms and Dominoes readers are available for you to download for your students from the Internet. (See 'Useful websites' on page 112.) You will need to join the Teacher's Club to access these as they are not available to students.

Recent developments in the delivery of digital reading materials make it inevitable that more reading in the future will be on screen rather than on paper.

Whether reading is done for the purposes of work, study, or pleasure, more and more of it already takes place on screen (and not just on computer screens), and this is likely to continue to increase over the coming years. Much reading now involves mobile phones and other similar devices. The development of the e-book means that many people are now reading literature on dedicated reading devices, like Amazon's Kindle.

Clearly much onscreen reading is not ER as we understand it. Nevertheless, increasingly, students are reading for pleasure on screen in their first language, and this clearly has the potential to carry over into second language reading. Browsing the web, which often involves pleasure reading, is also an interesting excursion away from the linear reading with which we are familiar.

How a digital library works

Essentially, a digital library operates in a way that mirrors a traditional library. Books can be borrowed and read, either online or downloaded. But because this takes place online, the experience is somewhat different.

To access a digital library, students sign in at a registration page which takes them to a library page. For a graded readers library, this is organized by level. If the students download a particular title, it will then appear in their own library page (often called a bookshelf). From there the students can open the book and read it on a computer, with the book appearing very much as it does on the printed page. Unlike the printed book, however, it is possible to add other features, and these may reinforce the attractions of digital libraries. The most attractive feature is simply the ability to play the audio and listen at the same time as reading. Other features include a facility for making notes on or around the text, for adding bookmarks, and for looking up words in a glossary. Finally, the reading can also link in to an online testing system.

It is expected that initially most digital libraries will be institutional. Schools or universities will subscribe on behalf of their students, giving them access to the library for a term or an academic year. Results of any test taken can feed into an institution's learning management system, and teachers can also monitor how many books their students are accessing.

Advantages of the digital library

The main advantage of a digital library is the improved access it can give students. Many institutions are geographically dispersed, making access to a traditional library quite a challenge. In addition, it should give students better access to a range of readers. In a traditional library, if one student has already borrowed a book, it is not available to other students. With a digital library there is no such constraint.

Selecting books is just as easy, if not easier, than with a traditional library. It is also generally easier for students who have chosen a book which they are not enjoying simply to return it to a digital library and select an alternative. This dedramatizes the whole selection process.

The digital system manages the students' access, so there is no library management for you, the teacher. And if the students are required to complete the tests, the monitoring of reading is also managed by the system.

Are students happy to read online?

In general, it seems that most students are happy to read online. Research in Japan has shown that students are just as comfortable reading on a computer or on a mobile phone as they are from a book. However, they would prefer to be using one of these devices (which they usually already own) than to invest in a specialist e-book. Research also shows that many students of English have rarely read books in their own language, whereas they probably have much more experience of both computers and mobile phones in their mother tongue. So we might expect an easier transfer to online reading in English.

Clearly the future of the digital library is still uncertain. But it may be a viable alternative to the traditional library, and it may also deliver reading material to students who have hitherto not enjoyed easy access.

Why this works

Giving students access to a library of graded readers is one of the most effective things you can do to improve their contact with English. It encourages them to continue their contact with the language outside the classroom, and it can significantly improve their motivation. Many teachers have found that the availability of self-selected reading materials becomes a high point for students, and improves the overall learning atmosphere of the classroom.

A library also develops students' ability to work autonomously, both in making choices over which book they are going to read and in choosing when and how they will actually read. This can be an important step in their further language development. In addition, those students who will need to read in English as part of their future studies will develop the necessary reading skills and stamina for it. The investment in a library can be one of the most positive decisions an English teacher can take.

6 Reading circles

Mark Furr

↓ WHAT ARE READING CIRCLES?

Reading circles are small groups of students who meet in the classroom to talk about the stories they have read. Reading circles provide two things that are often lacking in communication courses: first, reading material that is both comprehensible and interesting to talk about, and second, a framework in which having a real discussion in English is an achievable goal for students.

In all cultures, and for thousands of years, people have been fascinated by a good story – and language students are no exception. And a good story is at the very heart of every reading circle. Reading circles combine in a natural way the skills of reading, writing, speaking, and listening. They help motivate students to acquire the habit of reading extensively and working autonomously.

Teachers all over the world have been using **graded readers** for many years, asking their language students to read them outside of the classroom for **Extensive Reading** (ER) practice; and student enjoyment of graded readers is now well documented (Robb and Susser 1989; Elley 1991; Cho and Krashen 1994). Reading circles take advantage of this fact by moving graded readers into the classroom where they are used as core texts for discussion in reading circle groups.

Once students are engaged by a story, they are willing to give considerable thought to what they have read and make careful notes in order to be prepared for their group discussions. In their groups they are prepared to speak in English almost all of the time and to point out passages in a text in order to support their arguments. They also question each other in order to establish what the text really means. I call this level of engagement 'the magic of reading circles'.

↓ HISTORY OF READING CIRCLES

When learning about any new teaching concept, many teachers, myself included, will go online to see what they can discover about it. Any teacher doing a simple Internet search for 'reading circles' or 'literature circles' will find hundreds of pages relating to these terms. Almost all of these results will refer to material written on using literature/reading circles with native English-speaking (**L1**) students.

Before we discuss how to create the magic of reading circles in classrooms with foreign language (**L2**) students, let us first take a look at the history of literature/reading circles and how they originated and developed.

Reading circles for language students are based on the work of Harvey Daniels, an American teacher/researcher, and his colleagues in Chicago. In the 1980s, Daniels and his team were working with native English-speaking students in elementary, junior high, and high schools. They were trying to help students in economically disadvantaged school districts to improve their skills in English, especially in reading and writing. These teacher-researchers knew from years of experience that their L1 students cited reading and literature courses as their 'least favourite,' 'most difficult,' or 'most hated' courses in school, so Daniels set out to find an entirely new approach to teaching literature and reading classes. He and his colleagues realized that adults had enjoyed informal reading and book discussion together for hundreds of years, and as a result they decided to experiment with bringing the centuries-old tradition of talking informally about stories and books into elementary and secondary classes. In other words, they wanted to create informal student book clubs within the classroom itself.

However, when students were asked to read or study literature in a traditional school setting, the enjoyment, excitement, and passion that is often found in adult reading groups was sadly lacking. So Daniels and his colleagues began to hold student book club meetings in classrooms all over Chicago, and they called these classroom book clubs 'literature circles'.

Fortunately, the Daniels' group was helped along by the enormous popularity of television talk show host Oprah Winfrey's book clubs. About the time Daniels and his colleagues were launching literature circles in their Chicago classrooms, Winfrey gave both reading and literature a huge boost by hosting literature discussion groups on national television in the USA. Winfrey's discussion groups consisted of selected authors and ordinary members of the public. Winfrey's Book Club became so popular that soon adult book clubs were being formed all over the USA. People met in libraries, coffee shops, and in their homes to talk about literature. Suddenly, it was 'cool' to read literature and to talk about it with friends.

In Chicago, the timing was perfect. Daniels' literature circles proved to be highly successful as a means of engaging L1 students in their English classes and getting them to do the work necessary to improve their language skills. Daniels and his team documented their work in 1993 in *Literature Circles: Voice and Choice in Book Clubs and Reading Groups*. Since the publication of the book, literature circles have become extremely popular and are now used in L1 Language Arts classrooms throughout the USA. A revised edition of Daniels' book, published by Stenhouse in 2002, is recommended for anyone with an interest in the development of literature circles with L1 students.

As editor of the Oxford Bookworms Club: Stories for Reading Circles series, I must acknowledge that without the many years of research and hard work by Harvey Daniels and his colleagues, the Bookworms Club series (which introduces the concept of reading circles for use with English language students) would not exist. I should also like to acknowledge a presentation made by Pamela Bostelmann at the 2002 TESOL Arabia Conference in Abu Dhabi, UAE, where I was first exposed to the concept of literature circles.

At that point, I decided to try to introduce literature circles to my students in Japan. Back in Japan, I began to research the subject of literature circles. In doing so, I discovered that while a great deal had been written about using them in the L1 classroom in North America, very little had been written on using them with L2 students. I realized that if I was going to be successful in using literature circles with L2 students, I would need to carefully re-examine the standard model of literature circles as developed by Harvey Daniels and then to adapt this model for L2 students.

Daniels and his colleagues had created literature circles for use in elementary and secondary classrooms in the USA, but I would be using them to teach students who were not generally exposed to English in their everyday lives. Aside from the practice needed to become more fluent speakers of English, I knew that L2 students also need to work on building reading fluency as well as reading comprehension. Thus, a number of the primary assumptions used to create literature circles for L1 learners needed to be challenged if L2 teachers were to use this approach to teaching reading and discussion skills successfully.

↓ L1 LITERATURE AND L2 READING CIRCLES: DIFFERENCES

Since there has now been a great deal of research and information published on the use of the Daniels' model of literature circles, I think it is a good idea to take a clear look here at the differences and similarities between literature circles for L1 students and reading circles designed especially for use with non-native English-speaking (L2) students.

In *Literature Circles: Voice and Choice in Book Clubs and Reading Groups*, Daniels lists eleven key features essential for literature circles. I have no argument with his list of key elements for literature circles in L1 classes. However, at least three of the features, which Daniels defines as the most crucial for holding successful literature circles in L1 classes, need to be revised when used with L2 students.

First, a look at the three key elements which Daniels claims to be crucial to the success of L1 literature circles:

1 Students choose their own materials.
2 Small temporary groups are formed, based on book choice.
3 Different groups read different books.

Reading circles

I draw attention to these points because while I acknowledge that they are the central core of literature circles for use with L1 learners, these same points are those I knew needed to be revised when using this approach in L2 classrooms.

To conduct successful reading circles in the L2 classroom, I have replaced the first three of Daniels's key elements with the following:

1 Instructors select materials appropriate for their student population.
2 Small temporary groups are formed, based on student choice or the teacher's discretion.
3 Different groups are usually reading the same text.

Most of the changes I have made to the Daniels model of literature circles involve you, the teacher, setting texts at an appropriate level and pace for L2 language students. While Daniels insists that 'students choose their own materials' and read at their own pace, L2 language students need more guidance with choosing texts that are not too difficult and materials they are able to use as a basis for discussion in English.

For language students, the core of successful reading circles is the fact they allow students to participate in real-life, meaningful discussions about the stories they have read in English. Thus, it is important for you to choose materials at an appropriate level. Students should be able to read their reading circles texts without using a dictionary. A good way to find out whether a text is suitable for use in an L2 reading circle is to follow the recommendations for ER made by Waring and Takahashi (2000). Below are some good 'rules of thumb' for students to find their reading level:

 *Getting it right*

Find the right level

1 There should be no more than two or three unknown words per page.
2 The students are able to read eight to ten lines of text or more per minute.
3 The students understand almost all of what they are reading and with few pauses.

Remember, reading circles are based on the ability of our students, not only to read, but also to discuss the texts in English, so the materials must be manageable.

While Daniels insists that L1 students must be permitted to choose their own reading material, there are a number of reasons for L2 teachers to select the texts for their students. Most importantly, teachers need to select texts that are at an appropriate level and a suitable length for reading circles work. In most teaching situations, L2 students should not be reading more than 10–15 pages of text before they meet in groups for their reading circle discussion.

For ER practice, many L2 students may read a good deal more than 10–15 pages of a story at one sitting. However, here we are asking students to do some **close reading** of the text in order to prepare for their discussions in English; many students may want to read the story more than once before meeting in class for discussion. Thus, both the level and length of the assigned reading material must be manageable for students to have successful reading circle discussions in English in class.

Reading circles: classroom practice

Earlier we examined the differences in some of the key features between L1 literature circles and reading circles for L2 language students. Here we take a more detailed look at the nine key features I have identified for running successful L2 reading circles in the classroom:

✓ *Getting it right*

Apply the nine keys to successful reading circles

1   Select reading material appropriate for your student group.
    Reading circles require language learners to have real-life, meaningful discussions about the stories that they have read. It is important for you to choose appropriately graded reading texts, which your students can read without using a dictionary.

2   Create small temporary groups in the classroom.
    Setting a maximum of five to six students in a reading circle works best. At first, make sure that each group has one or two confident students who are willing to take a risk with something new.

3   Give different groups the same text to read.
    If each group reads the same story, these are the advantages:
    – it is much easier for you to monitor the progress of the discussion groups
    – it is possible to assign a number of different extension activities (including oral presentations and poster sessions, based on the story text)
    – you can evaluate students on their reading circles work by setting up extension activities and/or group projects
    – you may decide to give the students a mini lecture related to the story.

4   Organize your groups to meet on a regular, predictable basis to discuss their reading.
    This is a crucial aspect to the success of reading circles. Reading circles require some student training time, so you must be willing to devote time to trying out several stories and rounds of discussion if there are to be positive results.

5   Ask your students to use written notes to guide both their reading and their discussion.
    The role sheets (described below) prompt each member of the group to read a story from a different perspective, and to make notes in English in order to prepare for a group discussion based on their reading. In this way, students are learning that there are a number of different reasons for reading, and also different perspectives on any given text.

6   Ensure that the discussion topics come from the students.
    It is important to allow students to generate the topics for discussion. These are not classes in literary criticism, but informal discussions about stories. The role sheets provide the help needed for students to find interesting topics.

7 Allow the group meetings to be open, natural conversations about stories. Students are encouraged to share their opinions about the texts they read in the reading circles, so not all of the discussion will be too serious!

8 Be a facilitator, not a group member or 'teacher'.
You will need to step back and allow your students to assume responsibility for guiding the reading circle discussions. This is something you may not be used to, but as the students complete the role sheets in advance and know the roles that they are going to play in the group, it is important to allow this process to work freely and naturally.

9 Encourage a spirit of playfulness and fun to pervade the room.
Unless the reading circles are fun, we are simply repackaging the types of lessons that students tell us they hate. The goal of reading circles is clear and simple – to promote informal talk about great stories!

↓ GETTING STARTED WITH READING CIRCLES

Because choosing appropriate reading material is crucial to running successful reading circles, in this section we will quickly review the 'rules of thumb' for students to find their reading level, which are:

- There should be no more than two or three unknown words per page.
- The students are able to read eight to ten lines of text or more per minute.
- The students understand almost all of what they are reading and with few pauses.

It is usually a good idea to begin with a graded text that is one level below the student's current reading level as this helps to boost students' confidence and enjoyment of the activity.

Reading circle roles

Let us now look at the 'magic formula' for using reading circles with L2 students.

As stated earlier, reading circles are small groups of students who meet in the classroom to talk about stories. These groups allow language learners to have interesting discussions in English. And these discussions are made possible by the reading circles roles. Reading circles should be student-directed, but at the same time, our students need some tools in order to have enjoyable, interesting discussions about the stories they have read. These tools come in the form of the role sheets that students use when meeting in their groups. There are five basic roles for reading circles plus a sixth role for higher-level groups, which can be introduced later. These are:

1 discussion leader
2 summarizer
3 connector
4 word master
5 passage person
6 culture collector

To prepare for their roles, each student completes a role sheet. The role sheets break reading down into smaller sub-skills with each student focusing closely on one way of engaging with the text. Outside class, the students read the story from the perspective of their role. Then, when they come together in the reading circle, they use their role sheets as prompts for discussion, during which the different parts become the whole – in other words, the role sheets break down the skills of a mature reader into smaller, manageable parts so that each group member is responsible for one aspect of what a mature reader does naturally.

The student role sheets for each of the six roles discussed below can be found in the OUP Bookworms Club: Stories for Reading Circles Teacher's Handbook and are also available to download. (See 'Useful websites' on page 112.)

The first role is that of discussion leader, whose job is to act as a facilitator in the group and to keep the discussion flowing. Discussion leaders are asked to read the story a number of times so that they have a solid grasp of the basic plot of the story and other possible themes. They open the discussion with a few open-ended questions about the story and then ask other group members to share their findings with the group. The discussion leaders do not act as 'teacher'. Their job is to keep the conversation moving.

The second role is that of summarizer, whose task is to give a brief but complete summary of the plot. The idea here is for summarizers to understand that they are not to follow the text too closely; rather, they need to retell the story in their own words, choosing only the most important events in the narrative. When you introduce the summarizer role to your students, it is a good idea to suggest that the summarizer give their summary once, pause for a minute, then give it a second time.

The third role, the connector, is the one students often say is the most difficult when they first start working in reading circles. But by the end of a term, many students think that carrying out their role as the connector, and listening to their classmates in this role is the most interesting role of all. The connectors' role is to try to find connections between the text and the real world in which they live. When you introduce this role to students, explain that the connectors can focus on characters as well as events in the story. This is important, because in the case of stories such as mystery, horror, or adventure, students will rarely have had similar experiences. However, for nearly any type of story, the connectors may make connections between the thoughts, feelings, or actions of the characters in the story and their own lives, family members, friends, or classmates.

While the discussion leader, summarizer, and connector read the text and prepare to discuss the story from a global standpoint, the next two roles focus more closely on single words or very short phrases.

The fourth role is that of the word master. The word masters choose five words or short phrases which they believe to be the most important words in the story. The role of word master is not simply to choose and define unknown words. To make the role more interesting, encourage the students to look for special uses of common words and to ask their group members questions such as *What do you think _____ means in this situation?* or *Why do you think the writer repeats the word _____ eight times in the first two pages of this story?* Explain that the word master should use an English/English learner's dictionary when defining words for this role.

The fifth of the core roles is that of the passage person. The role of the passage person is to choose at least three passages in the story that are important for the plot, that explain the characters, or that use interesting or powerful language. The passage person comments on each of the selected passages and asks the group one or two questions about each passage. Encourage the passage person to choose puzzling or difficult passages and to ask the group for help in understanding them. Some of the best discussion occurs when the students are trying to figure out the meaning of difficult passages together.

The sixth role (that you should only use with more advanced groups) is that of the culture collector. During the development of reading circles for L2 students, this role was created in response to the frequent struggles students had with the cultural issues and historical backgrounds of some of the stories used in reading circles. Having one student focus on cultural issues later in the term adds a further level of interest and complexity to the discussions. Only introduce this role when your students are comfortable with their reading circle activities and roles and then only with intermediate students and above.

The culture collectors' job is to look at the story and note both differences and similarities between the culture represented in the story and their own culture. Remind your culture collector that 'culture' may include customs, traditions, and everyday life. Again, it is a good idea to encourage the culture collector to choose passages with a puzzling cultural reference. The group can then work together to understand unfamiliar cultural issues in the story. This role and the connector role have this in common – they both look for connections. The connector finds connections with personal experience, while the culture collector compares and contrasts cultures and looks for cross-cultural connections.

Introducing the roles in class

The magic behind reading circles lies in the role sheets, which guide students through their reading, and make it easy for them to prepare for discussion in English about the stories they have read. So it is important first to spend some class time introducing the roles and the role sheets clearly to students.

Try this ☞ **Introduce the roles**

1 First, explain the purpose of the roles. Then put the students into groups of five or six. (These will become the first reading circle groups.) Try to make sure that there are at least two confident students in each group.

2 Give each student a set of the six role sheets, taken from the Bookworms Club Teacher's Handbook or downloaded from the Internet. (See 'Useful websites' on page 112.)

3 Introduce the first five roles at this point, but wait until the second or third session of reading circles before introducing the sixth role (the culture collector) to your more advanced groups.

4 Present each role, one at a time, pausing after each one. Allow students time to discuss among themselves in their groups, to consolidate their understanding of the role.

5 Encourage your students to write notes on the role sheets, which they can keep and refer to later when they are assigned a particular role.

6 After you have presented the five/six roles, give the students a photocopy of the role sheet examples. Two samples are given below. Further photocopiable samples for each role can be found in the Reading Circles Teacher's Handbook and as a download. (See 'Useful websites' on page 112.) After they have looked at the completed sample role sheets, invite students to write down a few questions about the roles. You could then write these questions on the board and elicit answers from other groups in the class.

W Word Master   **STORY:** *The Christmas Presents*

MY WORDS	MEANING OF THE WORD	REASON FOR CHOOSING THE WORD
One dollar and eighty-seven cents. PAGE _4_ LINE _1 - 8_	This is a small amount of money in the U.S.	This tells us how poor they are and shows us that Della thinks she needs to buy something as a gift for her husband.
curls PAGE _6_ LINE _14_	These are little rings of hair.	Della was worried about her curls. We think curls are cute. So I don't understand why she was worried. Perhaps, in the story's time, only straight hair was beautiful.

C Connector   **STORY:** *The Christmas Presents*

MY CONNECTIONS:

1 I was moved by this story because I remember that giving a present to someone is not important. But our heart and mind is important when we try to give a present. When I was an elementary school student, I gave my father a present. I carefully made a very small stuffed toy cat. I sewed it with felt. Then, I wrote a short letter to my father and put it into the cat's mouth. "Finished, I did it." But when I saw my workmanship again, it looked ugly and careless. The next day was my father's birthday. I gave the failure to him, but he was very pleased! I couldn't understand it. But as the years passed, the more I understood it. I am much older, but my father still has my ugly cat. I noticed that he received not my present, but my heart at that time. This is the same feeling that Jim and Della have when they get the presents that are useless.

FIGURE 6.1   *Role sheet examples from Bookworms Club Teacher's Handbook*

Reading and role sheet preparation

After your introductory session on role sheets, here are some other useful things you can do to help prepare students for reading circles.

✓ *Getting it right*

Prepare reading schedules and role sheets

1 The students make or fill in their own copy of a reading schedule. They write the names of their group members, and the role each member will play during the discussion meeting. For the Bookworms Club model of reading circles, photocopiable reading schedules are available in the Bookworms Club Teacher's Handbook or as a pdf file. (See 'Useful websites' on page 112.)

2 With younger or lower-level students, both the reading and the role sheet preparation can be done in class. However, most students usually read the entire short story and complete their role sheet in English for homework in preparation for the discussion meeting.

3 Explain to your students that their role sheets will be used as notes for discussion, so they have to use vocabulary and structures that their classmates will understand. Advise students not to use a dictionary while completing their role sheets unless it is an English/English learner's dictionary.

4 Encourage students, before coming to class, to practise reading their role sheets notes aloud to themselves. Emphasize that their written notes are there to help with the discussion.

5 In some teaching situations, it is a good idea to tell students that even if they are absent on the day of the reading circle meeting, they should still have their work ready and give it to another group member to present it for them in class. Making students responsible for their roles, whether or not they are in class, not only promotes student responsibility but also a very high attendance rate. When students realize that they have to complete the assignment whether they are present or not, they often decide that it is easier to come to class and participate than arrange to send in their homework by proxy!

Group discussions

Discussion in small groups of five or six may be new for many students. For the first reading circle session, it is a good idea to allow only 30–40 minutes of discussion time. This should be enough for each group to go through all the roles and have time for follow-up questions and comments. The goal is to finish before the students have exhausted their enthusiasm for discussion, so that they will be motivated to try reading circles again.

For those interested in the Bookworms Club model of reading circles, the Bookworms Club Teacher's Handbook provides additional information, including answers to some 'Frequently Asked Questions' (FAQs), suggestions for a number of expansion activities, and instructions for using reading circles with longer texts.

Why this works

As I said earlier in this chapter, I believe that reading circles are magic. For language students, this magic works in a number of ways. First, students feel as if they are having interesting, important discussions in English during their participation in reading circles. I contend that because the reading circle role sheets give each group of students a set of clear (though complex) tasks, they are able to have discussions at a far deeper level than those commonly heard in L2 classrooms that use coursebooks or discussion-based textbooks. The magic lies in the fact that the sum of these role sheets is far greater (and more complex and interesting) than any of the individual parts. Second, reading circles are magic because at the heart lies something mentioned on the first page of this chapter – a good story. We all know that students enjoy reading graded readers, and reading circles serve to relocate ER materials from the periphery of the language classroom to its centre.

References

Cho, K. and **S. D. Krashen.** 1994. 'Acquisition of vocabulary from the Sweet Valley Kids series: adult ESL acquisition.' *Journal of Reading 37*: 662–7.

Daniels, H. 2002. *Literature Circles: Voices and Choice in Book Clubs and Reading Groups* (2nd edn.). Portland, ME: Stenhouse.

Elley, W. B. 1991. 'Acquiring literacy in a second language: the effect of book-based programs'. *Language Learning 41*.

Furr, M. 2009. *Bookworms Club Reading Circles* Teacher's Handbook (2nd edn.). Oxford: Oxford University Press.

Robb, T. N. and **B. Susser.** 1989. 'Extensive reading vs skills building in an EFL context.' *Reading in a Foreign Language 5*: 239–251.

Waring, R. and **Takahashi, S**. 2000. *The Why and How of Using Graded Readers.* Toyko: Oxford University Press.

Part 3   Extensive Reading: case studies

7

An Extensive Reading Programme in Jordan

Nina Prentice

Most Jordanians are acutely aware that English is vital not only to gain entry to university but also to access the best jobs, particularly in the private sector. In recent years, the Jordanian Government has worked hard to improve English teaching and learning, instigating many initiatives to address the quality and methods of instruction. However, despite efforts to update textbooks, establish schools for the most able, and introduce a comprehensive e-curriculum programme, many children in the state sector struggle with English. A number of factors in the following areas contributed to this situation at the time of the project:

First, curriculum and assessment:

Close government supervision of state schools ensured that each year group received the relevant authorized textbook and that teachers delivered it systematically. Students and teachers worried that any departure from tried and tested routines could affect preparation for assessment. This was a serious concern because all test material was taken directly from each year's coursebook. The role of the students was to memorize the textbooks. Total recall guaranteed successful results in examinations (but few practical English skills!).

Second, learning environment:

- **Large classes:** State sector classrooms were often basic and overcrowded. The average class size was around forty-five students but groups of fifty or more were not uncommon. In fact, two classes with over sixty children participated in the programme.
- **Social profile and ability:** The socio-economic mix of these schools was broad. Backgrounds ranged from middle-class children to students who lived in refugee camps or came from nomadic families. Classes were single sex and divided into a less able 'literary stream' and higher-ability 'scientific stream'.
- **Teaching methods:** High numbers and the broad ability range in classes made it difficult to use communicative teaching methods. Many classrooms also lacked the audiovisual resources to maximize the benefit of this kind of teaching. As a result, many teachers relied on traditional approaches.
- **Students:** Most Jordanian students were keen to do well but there were significant gender differences in their attitude to learning. Girls were more willing to try out new strategies, while most boys believed that they would succeed in examinations by faithful memorization of the textbook.

- **Teachers:** Jordanian teachers worked with over-large classes, heavy teaching timetables, and an overloaded syllabus. There were also significant gender differences in teaching style. Women teachers generally welcomed new ideas about teaching, while male colleagues relied heavily on rote learning. They justified this approach by claiming that these routines were what both their students and their parents wanted.

↓ WHY CHOOSE AN EXTENSIVE READING PROGRAMME?

Despite having studied English for more than 1,700 hours over at least eight years, most Jordanian eighteen-year-olds sitting the 2004 school leaving examination had few practical English skills to show for their efforts. It also seemed unjust that private school candidates, benefiting from better resources and more intensive English teaching both inside and out of school, were better placed in the competition for university places and future employment. The well-documented evidence of the benefits of **Extensive Reading** (ER) suggested that it could have the same impact on learners struggling in the Jordanian state sector.

The resulting Extensive Reading Programme (ERP) had six main objectives:

- **Broadening exposure to English:** ER would provide practice in English outside the limitations of textbook tasks and exam preparation. Rigid, traditional teaching routines undermined most students' ability to use the language in real-life situations. It was felt that a Jordanian version of ER could reinforce existing knowledge as well as introduce new vocabulary and syntax in a natural way. A selling point of the programme was that twenty minutes' extensive reading per day for six days a week was the equivalent of a free weekly two-hour private lesson with a native speaker!
- **Establishing critical reading and thinking skills:** Jordanian students could memorize the syllabus for examination but had little experience of open questions or discussion and debate. Moreover, successful traditional learning entailed not only memorization of the syllabus but also comprehensive recall of the teacher's authorized interpretation. The central aim of the ERP was to introduce both students and their teachers to texts freed from the tyranny of the textbook. The stories in the readers were not official. Like television programmes, they could be liked or disliked. Reasoned argument based on textual evidence was the goal – no one would be obliged to agree with an 'authorized' version.
- **Stimulating learner independence by encouraging a love of reading:** Few Jordanians read for pleasure. Books in school and university were rote-learned for examination. The ERP wanted learners to experience books as enjoyable and entertaining. Once students recognized the power that books have to be both pleasurable and useful, it was hoped that a passion for reading and interest in lifelong learning would follow.

- **Extending learning opportunities for girls:** Local custom meant that Jordanian girls were less free than boys to seek entertainment and opportunities outside the home. The ERP was to be a good resource for girls to develop their skills and knowledge without disrupting traditional expectations.

- **Developing student-centred teaching resources to reinforce syllabus objectives:** In order to be successful in Jordan, the ERP had to address three issues:
  1 The programme had to satisfy the Ministry of Education that it was a rigorous initiative with quantifiable results.
  2 It must minimize any extra work that might be imposed on teachers' already heavy timetables.
  3 It had to help students in their task of learning an overloaded syllabus.

  To meet these challenges, it was essential to engage the active participation of teachers. They were to be encouraged, together with their students, to find workable ways of exploiting ER in their classrooms. At the same time, students and teachers also needed to explore the best ways of encouraging reading, and monitoring its progress. All new developments were to be shared at training sessions where teachers also devised the assessments necessary to satisfy the Ministry's need for quantifiable results.

- **Enhancing teachers' language skills and developing their autonomy in the classroom:** Many Jordanian teachers' grasp of English was limited. The necessity for teachers involved in ER to familiarize themselves with their class libraries meant that they, too, would have to practise reading as much if not more than their students. Running an ERP in their classrooms would also provide opportunities for devising teaching strategies and materials and then reflecting on them. It was hoped that experiencing English outside the limitations of the curriculum and participating in ongoing training sessions on different aspects of ER would develop these teachers' linguistic and pedagogic confidence.

↓ SETTING UP THE EXTENSIVE READING PROGRAMME

Agreeing a book list

It was not difficult to get initial agreement for a pilot ERP from the Minister of Education. However, it took far longer to secure the Ministry's authorization for a list of titles for the project, because there were concerns that some of the texts might be inappropriate in an Islamic context. Officials had to be persuaded that neither the books nor their values would be explicitly 'taught' but were simply part of a voluntary reading programme designed to improve students' English skills. The final agreed list was heavily based on pre-20th century classics and non-fiction. Despite the lack of contemporary material, the books proved a good choice because students and teachers found it easy to relate their values to those in the texts.

An Extensive Reading Programme in Jordan

Fund raising

A combination of charity fundraising organized by the British Embassy together with OUP's support secured the necessary resources to buy 15 class libraries. British Council and British Embassy backing also meant that the project had credibility not only with the Ministry but also with senior Jordanians. Their interest in the ERP meant that finding funds for its development between 2004 and 2006 was never a serious challenge.

Training plan

A total of 15 teachers were trained in two batches over two semesters. After a review of the purpose and methods of ER, the focus of the sessions was on the practicalities of running the programme in a Jordanian context. From the very beginning it was clear that the only way ER would work in Jordan was to tailor it to support the teaching and learning of the syllabus for each year group. It was also essential to convince everyone in the school community, including teachers, students, parents, and administrators, that regularly practising reading and using the books as a class resource would deliver significantly improved examination results, as well as better general English skills.

Libraries

Teachers took charge of their libraries immediately, reading as many of the books as possible before the beginning of the semester. Libraries were the responsibility of the ER-trained teachers and were expected to follow them if they moved schools. However, it was agreed that if teachers left state sector teaching, their books would be returned to the British Council and reallocated to new teachers recruited to the programme.

Storage

Because it was important that the books be accessible and not locked up out of reach in school libraries, the teachers decided on secure library cabinets, one for each class, to maximize access for their ER students.

Lending

Early on in training, various systems for monitoring lending and dealing with book loss and damage were discussed. While teachers were ultimately answerable for their libraries, it was agreed that day-to-day administration of the books would depend upon rotas of student librarians. Despite initial doubts, teachers were delighted with their students' enthusiastic and conscientious supervision of the libraries.

Administrative support

The ERP relied heavily on the Ministry's and school heads' backing for the programme. Senior officials were positive about the project and regularly went out of their way to resolve problems as they arose. School heads were also helpful, particularly when they began to see the programme in action and the positive effect it was having on students. It was at more junior levels in the Ministry that difficulties sometimes occurred. However, although teachers were discouraged by these setbacks, it was much to their credit that they remained thoroughly committed to the programme.

Training sessions

Throughout the pilot, the teachers' input was central to the ERP. Although meetings were often argumentative, there was a strong sense of loyalty to the programme. Teachers were keen to share successful practice with colleagues and show off their students' ER work. Their critical evaluations of the programme and thorough 'road testing' of resources developed throughout the pilot helped maximize the impact of ER. Despite the huge institutional and practical challenges, most teachers found innovative ways of overcoming the main enemy of the programme – lack of time to cover the official textbook for the examinations.

Below are some of the ER strategies devised by the teachers. These made it possible to complete the syllabus while checking up on students' reading.

- **Textbook answer sheet:** Textbook homework was usually reviewed orally in class and often took up a significant proportion of the lesson. One teacher typed up a daily answer sheet and posted it in the classroom, inviting students to check their answers during breaks. She then used the time freed up for ER activities.
- **Minute paper:** Students were given one minute to write a description of a character, place, or topic in one of The Oxford Bookworms Library readers (for example, *Macbeth*, *New York*, or *Food and Drink in Britain*). The teacher who devised this activity used it as a 'starter' to motivate his class of eleven-year-old boys and tailored it to focus on particular syllabus objectives. He found that students' writing improved dramatically as a result of regular practice of these short, timed tasks.
- **ER relative clauses:** The teacher wrote the title of a book with which most of the class was familiar on the board beside a list of relative pronouns. Students were invited to work in mixed-ability groups to create complex sentences about events or characters in the story. The task was competitive and timed. Groups were rewarded for finishing first or producing the most 'true' sentences about the story or including the most interesting facts about it. The task worked equally well with a focus on different grammatical points.
- **Present simple passive:** Another teacher found that teaching the passive voice was a lot simpler when students recognized its purpose looking at recipes in *Food and Drink in Britain* and using it to write their own recipes for typical Jordanian dishes.
- **Heroes' and heroines' routines:** One teacher reinforced a textbook task on daily routines by asking a student to describe in the first person the daily routine of a particular individual in the book she was reading. Classmates then enjoyed guessing the name of the character and the title of the book.

More challenging tasks which teachers created to develop problem solving, analytical thinking, and critical reading skills included:

- **Data show:** Students were invited to create PowerPoint presentations linking curriculum topics like 'Women in the Workforce' to the ER texts. This worked particularly well because learners did not just practise IT skills and effective oral presentation. Research on female authors in the ER library (all of whom were born before 1900!) and exploration of attitudes towards them allowed students to consider society's reaction to women who break out of traditional roles.
- **Peer teaching:** Students were asked to create their own resources to exploit ER. They produced many different examples of comprehension exercises, vocabulary and grammar revision tasks, and mock examination papers based on Bookworms titles.
- **Role-play:** In one class, a group of more able girls set up a simulated television broadcast to gather student views on the ERP. The 'talk show hosts' devised *Wh-* questions which less confident students answered, taking on a variety of roles as parents, teachers, and students. Even the weakest students forgot their inhibitions about responding in English in the enjoyment of role-play.
- **ER newsletter:** One teacher helped her class to publish a regular newsletter to record their reading. Items included book reviews, winners of weekly ER challenges, games based on ER texts, 'interviews' with characters in books and 'reports' on incidents in stories, as well as creative writing and illustration inspired by stories. These activities provided opportunities for all abilities in the class. The newsletter was posted in the corridor for the whole school to enjoy.
- **Questionnaires:** A number of teachers in the pilot invited students to create questionnaires about different features of the programme. This task addressed a broad range of skills. Practical application of grammar and vocabulary knowledge was necessary to draft the questions. Determining how to elicit relevant data and then present it in an informative way involved complex cross-curricular thinking and problem-solving skills.
- **Drama:** Another successful strategy much enjoyed by most students was the opportunity ER gave them to experiment with drama. Classes were invited to use Bookworms stories as inspiration to write and perform their own plays. There was huge enthusiasm for this activity and some excellent plays were produced in the course of the pilot.
- **ER festival:** During the spring semester, teachers noted that students' worries about upcoming examinations were stopping many from reading. A group of teachers came up with the idea of having a festival to celebrate students' work on the project and persuade them not to drop good reading habits in favour of revision. Competitions were organized in a variety of categories, to encourage everyone to participate. The response was overwhelming and those students with active and innovative teachers achieved fantastic results in all areas regardless of age, ability, or class size.

Try this ☞ **Experiment with new activities**

In your own ERP you may like to try out some of the activities listed above with your students.

Testing

The programme had to deliver a quantifiable evaluation of its impact on students. The teachers decided to use data collected with end-of-pilot tests contrasted with the results of control groups who had not practised ER. In an effort to give a comprehensive picture of the effect of the ERP on student progress, the tests were designed to consist of a combination of comprehension, cloze, thinking skills, and writing elements. Because this kind of testing was new to most of the students, teachers familiarized them with the format by administering a set of six tests of increasing difficulty (Bookworms levels 1–6).

Certification of teachers

The Ministry required that teachers' participation in training and their delivery of ER in the classroom be closely monitored throughout the pilot. Teacher assessment included observations, a written assignment, a final examination, and submission of a portfolio of student work. On successful completion of all these stages, the British Council awarded teachers training certificates recognized by the Ministry. This was an important incentive for participating teachers.

Parents

There was some anxiety that parents might object to some of the fiction in the libraries. During initial training, teachers informed and reassured parents about the aims of the ERP. The thrust of the briefings was to emphasize that the programme was about choice not compulsion and that children could read as much or as little as they wished. ER readers used in class would not be textbooks to be taught and memorized, rather, the books would be starting points for discussion, debate, and thinking skills activities.

↓ THE BENEFITS OF THE EXTENSIVE READING PROGRAMME

Evaluation

The Ministry's need for quantifiable results to gauge the programme's impact meant that considerable time and effort went into designing and administering the end-of-pilot tests described above. Students from both semester cohorts participated between March and May of 2006 alongside control groups who had not practised ER.

The results provided solid evidence that ER had a significant overall effect on student performance both in reading comprehension as well as in writing and thinking skills. ER students outperformed both their peers and older classes who had not participated in the programme by an average of 17 per cent in cloze and reading comprehension and 14 per cent in thinking skills and writing.

Over and above the evidence of the tests, the ERP had less quantifiable but perhaps more important impact in the areas listed below.

Written work

The scale of the voluntary written response to the ERP was unexpectedly large. Teachers regularly submitted huge portfolios of students' work for discussion in the workshops. The work was varied, ranging from stories, poems, and drama inspired by the books, to reading comprehension exercises for testing fellow students. There were also many IT projects, some of considerable originality and quality.

Some teachers felt overwhelmed by the scale of student response and worried about the time needed to review and acknowledge students' efforts. A solution was to use class displays of written work to reward those who had made exceptional efforts and to encourage others to contribute. This was an effective strategy in motivating students and raising awareness of the ERP throughout the school community.

Writing is always difficult to teach, even to native speakers. Nevertheless, the ERP provided a wide range of opportunities for students to experiment and develop their writing, both within the syllabus and outside it. Anyone starting an ERP in a similar context would do well to include a strong writing focus in the teacher training.

Classroom observations

Throughout the pilot there were numerous observations of participating classes. Their purpose was to record learning strategies, student–teacher interaction, assimilation of training objectives, and student reactions to ER resources.

One striking development was the extent to which students became responsible and effective teachers of their peers. Teachers often asked their classes to plan and teach ER lessons. Students were enthusiastic and devised many imaginative tasks based on Bookworms texts. The impact of these opportunities on the quality of learning was a revelation to teachers.

Students also enjoyed thinking skills challenges and welcomed the change of pace and focus which ER activities provided. One group used their reading to make extensive links with issues raised by campaigners in their textbook, by reviewing how many of the books had themes focused on minority rights. An impressive number of connections were made, beyond the obvious choices of *Martin Luther King* and *Cry Freedom*. Some of these connections included:

1 *Robin Hood* and *A Tale of Two Cities* = injustice to the poor
2 *The Little Princess*, *Oliver Twist*, and *David Copperfield* = the maltreatment and exploitation of children
3 *The Elephant Man* and *Frankenstein* = prejudice towards the disabled
4 *Animals in Danger* and *Black Beauty* = cruelty and exploitation of animals
5 *The Scarlet Letter* = injustice towards women, and double standards.

The quality of students' discussion and their ability to use evidence, connect ideas, argue, and problem solve was impressive.

Approximately five per cent of participating students were exceptionally keen, and read their entire library (approximately 120 books – over a million words!) in the course of the year, although on average most students read five books per semester. As the programme developed, it was clear that ER provided a range of activities, from simple oral book reports to student-driven activities. These allowed learners to participate with increasing confidence in lessons as real users of language. As one teacher put it, his boys '…were enthusiastic, happy, and were waiting for the ER lesson more than for any other'.

Teacher–student interaction

Teachers and students quickly recognized the impact that ER was having on learning. Teachers observed that regular readers' test results improved significantly and that they were better than non-readers at answering reading comprehension questions, especially those which required more detailed explanations.

However, it was the cooperation and mutual understanding of teachers and students, fostered by their shared reading, that was one of the ERP's most positive outcomes. One teacher observed:

> ER built bridges between me and my students and the parents, too. Moreover, the programme discovered many hidden abilities in my students and it also helped me discover them.

Another teacher noted:

> Everyone in the scheme felt the human relationships between teacher and student. My students felt that I am a human before being a teacher, and I felt that my students are so human that they need a lot of polite treatment in order to give.

Teacher development

The majority of teachers on the pilot were hardworking and committed during training and throughout the delivery of the pilot. Although improvements in their language and pedagogic skills were anticipated, the extent of progress exceeded all expectations. Regular reading, reflection, written work, and discussion in English supported their development as much as that of their students. Many remarked on how much more confident they had become as teachers and speakers of English as a result of ER. Most said that they had really enjoyed reading the libraries and hoped to keep up reading in English.

Parents and families

Despite initial anxieties, parents became enthusiastic supporters of the programme and its impact on their children's progress. As one teacher reported, 'One parent told me that his daughter grew and changed her behaviour to become an adult.' A number of teachers mentioned that students shared books with their parents and siblings, often translating the stories into Arabic for them. In fact, in many classes the ERP became a 'family programme' with regular readings and discussion of the stories at home.

Why this works

Within the Ministry-defined objectives of the pilot, the ERP helped students improve their English skills and examination results. However, its most significant contribution was to create humanized classrooms where students and teachers worked together as communities of learners. ER also had a powerful cross-curricular influence. In the autumn semester following the pilot, a teacher reported that her previous year's ER group impressed their Arabic and Islamic Studies teachers with their capacity to assimilate ideas and understand and discuss complex texts. The ability of ER students to transfer critical learning skills to other academic subjects points to the formative influence regular reading and debate can have on learners.

ER is undeniably powerful, but it is the teachers who are vital to the implementation of any educational reform. They have the responsibility for delivering new ideas in the classroom convincingly and they must be given a voice rather than have yet more external initiatives imposed upon them. Indeed, this group's main recommendation was to increase the impact and effectiveness of ER by giving it official status in the curriculum with timetabled lessons.

Nevertheless, the main reason this project worked so well was its democratic and collaborative approach. Throughout the pilot, teachers participated actively in the regular training sessions. They frankly shared experiences, both positive and negative, and worked together to forge the best practice. This teamwork allowed teachers to play a fundamental role in adapting ER in practical ways to the realities of the Jordanian classroom, thereby giving their students genuine tools to improve their English language skills.

8 The Extensive Reading Programme in Bahrain

Minas Mahmood

Unquestionably, learning a foreign language is not an easy task for many students. It is a challenge which requires great motivation, dedication, and commitment. In order for students to succeed, teachers not only need an updated knowledge of the methodology of language teaching, but also need to draw upon a range of teaching strategies that increase students' motivation and enhance their language skills.

One of these strategies is **Extensive Reading** (ER) – reading stories to develop students' language skills. In a variety of contexts, research has confirmed that students' language skills (reading, writing, listening, and speaking) improve when they read stories. Research also confirms that reading stories has a motivational impact on students. When students select and read materials suitable to their language levels and can identify with the story, they feel more encouraged to read, and consequently gain a sense of achievement. Reading stories is also an effective means of exposing EFL students to the target language culture. Classical stories transmit the culture of the people about whom the stories were written. By learning about the culture, students learn about the past and the present, about people's customs and traditions. Culture teaches students to understand others and respect their differences. This is an important area that the Ministry of Education in Bahrain attempts to foster, not only in the Civic Education curriculum but in other school subjects as well. A further important benefit of using stories is to enhance students' critical thinking skills. Students read, discuss, and analyse what they read. As a result, they develop a wider range of vocabulary, increase their cultural knowledge, and develop a more positive attitude towards literature and their language learning.

With these benefits in mind, when Oxford University Press approached the Ministry of Education in Bahrain with a proposal to pilot an Extensive Reading Programme (ERP), the Ministry embraced the idea and felt that the programme would serve our needs at two different levels:

1 First, it would create an opportunity for schools to explore a different way of supporting the language needs of learners and also create an opportunity to study the impact of the programme on students' language development.
2 Second, it would constitute a professional development opportunity for our secondary teachers, in that they would be trained by collaborator–experts on how to implement the programme and experiment with different strategies to maximize the programme's effectiveness for our students.

The Extensive Reading Pilot Project was initiated in Bahrain's secondary schools at the end of October 2007. A number of **graded readers** were placed in grade 10 of 15 secondary classrooms with the aim of assessing the impact of ER on students' acquisition of English. (The secondary level in Bahrain covers grades 10–12, serving students aged 15–18.)

An additional aim of the pilot was to trial three different approaches to implementing ER in order to evaluate which would be most beneficial to learners. Oxford University Press supplied the readers together with a range of support materials, including a CD-Rom of project support documents. Students were given a placement test at the beginning of the project to help teachers identify their level and provide them with suitable books. It was planned to conduct a post-pilot test at the end of the academic year in December 2008 to establish what gains in language learning, if any, had taken place.

To this end, some schools were given the materials to implement the Class Readers approach (discussed in Chapter 4), where all the students read the same book; other schools received 45 different titles for a class of 30 students to implement the Class Libraries approach (discussed in Chapter 5); and the remaining schools received readers in sets of six to enable teachers to form six groups in order to work with the Reading Circles approach (discussed in Chapter 6).

The schools were selected on the basis of their willingness to participate in this exploratory project – they were not mandated to use it. Therefore, the necessary first step was to familiarize schools with the nature of the project and help them to understand how to implement it successfully. Teachers needed to be well prepared and provided with the necessary techniques for working with the project. The project began with a four-day training session, involving 30 teachers from 15 secondary schools. Initially it was thought that once teachers received the introductory training, they would be ready to start the reading project. However, this was not quite as easy as anticipated.

As with any innovation, not all schools were able to carry out the project smoothly at first. At the initial stage, teachers allocated part of their classroom time to the ER project (usually 15 minutes of their language class time). This was manageable for those who were able to plan their core course lessons and incorporate the ER element into their lesson plan. Others, however, viewed the project as a task over and above their teaching load and did not feel able to begin the project immediately. Teachers who did start were satisfied with the way students were responding to the project and collaborating with their teachers. These teachers also noted an increase in the students' affective relationship with the English language: they became more motivated to study English because they saw the immediate benefits – in terms of enjoyment – that ER brought to them.

It became clear that close monitoring would be necessary to learn more about the experiences of the various schools, and to provide support and guidance for the teachers. At this stage, Oxford University Press greatly assisted us in giving teachers the help and support they needed for the early stages of the pilot. My colleague from Oxford University Press offered to collaborate with me, and we conducted a number of classroom visits together. These visits became very important for a number of reasons. The outcome of these joint visits was that we were able to:

- find out how schools were implementing and coping with the project
- provide ongoing support to those teachers who expressed concerns
- put teachers in touch with more experienced colleagues
- advise teachers on how to get assistance from those teachers who were running their pilot more successfully.

It became clear that in attempting to help schools to cope with innovation (in this case introducing ER as a means of improving students' language ability and fostering more positive learning practices), and to make teachers feel comfortable and able to accept the new approach, it was necessary to provide continuous support for the teachers. This took the form of:

- short training sessions offered by our collaborators
- classroom visits
- regular teachers' meetings, in which the group reflected on their experiences and shared ideas and suggestions on how to manage certain difficulties and overcome obstacles.

The resulting networking created a community of teachers committed to making the ER programme more successful in their own schools and to working harder to help their students become better readers.

↓ STAKEHOLDERS' FEEDBACK

As the end of term approached, teachers started reporting feedback from students. Some of the teachers on the project managed it more effectively as a result of feedback from their students; others were still struggling and had barely managed to structure their classes to accommodate ER at all.

A meeting was therefore arranged to address the various concerns and to explore options to help teachers manage the project more successfully. At this meeting, teachers raised practical problems (such as lack of time to finish the tasks during the lesson). Teachers in boys' schools, particularly, pointed out that they needed more lower-levels readers. All the teachers present emphasized the need to allocate a full period to ER in order for students to benefit more from their Reading Circles.

In subsequent meetings, some teachers asked for more support from the Ministry. They felt that they were getting positive results from the students and that more time should be dedicated to reading. We therefore approached the Directorate of Secondary Education at the Ministry to request more time allocation, describing the current project and highlighting its benefits to students and asking for their cooperation and support. As a result, at the end of the 2008 academic year, the Ministry agreed to allocate three periods a week to all schools with an ERP. These three periods are usually earmarked for Extra Curricular Activities but can be used for any innovative project. This constituted formal recognition of the importance of the project in furthering English language skills.

During the second and third year of the project, we continued to hold regular meetings with participating schools once a term to discuss their needs and concerns. It became evident that school teachers were becoming increasingly competent in the ERP and that this was having a positive impact on colleagues who were not involved in the project.

In this context, I would like to recount one of the success stories from a school involved in the ERP since 2007. (In order to protect her identity, we have called the teacher who shared her personal account of the project, 'Najah'. Here is her account of her experience with the ERP.) [All indented quotations below are given verbatim.]

The Extensive Reading Programme: a success story in my school

Ever since I was a student myself, I had always been passionate about reading. Years later when I decided to study English at the University, I felt that the best way to improve my own language was to read and continue reading more, fortunately I was right.

Since my appointment as an English language teacher, I have tried to get my students into reading, especially short stories. But it was really hard, and I could not even make it as part of their classroom projects. Years later, my dream came true when I was introduced to the Extensive Reading Programme and received training on how to implement the programme in my classrooms.

As one of the pilot schools, my school received resources that were enough to implement the Circle's Approach rather than the Class Readers' Approach. In addition to the core courses that I had been assigned to teach, I was also given two different groups of students as part of "Creativity Hours". These are three periods a week allocated for extra curricular activities. I decided to start with a small number of students (15), which would make it easier for me to motivate, monitor and train.

I decided to use the "Creativity Hours" to apply Extensive Reading Programme with my remedial group. These were students whose level of English is considered very low. Most of the students who joined the programme had never had previous experience with extensive reading in English ...

Acting as a model and talking about my personal experience as a bookworm was the spell that made my students read. I knew that it can be hard to understand the characters' attitudes in the classical stories. So I talked briefly about some medieval issues showing how interesting they are, especially those which are related to marriage which female students usually enjoy reading about. I guess that contributed in making reading classics more interesting for my students.

As I reflect back on my three-year experience with implementing Extensive Reading Programme, I realize not only my students' learning habits have improved but also they have benefited from the programme in several, ways. These changes I observed through their writing and class discussions

The Extensive Reading Programme in Bahrain

and through our continuous dialogues together in the class as part of my formative assessment. From their comments, I have learned that my students now enjoy reading and feel it has shaped their personalities and has improved their attitudes towards learning English.

Moreover, the habit of reading is very contagious. So once students gave up the best of their teenage hobbies for the sake of enjoying reading a story, we started having more fun in the class. Actually some of my students used to invite their friends from other classes who were curious and wanted to know more about the interesting events and characters that they had heard my students talk about. Even some of them also started borrowing stories for their sisters at home. I have also learned that even some of their siblings have become addicted to reading ...

Another factor which contributed to motivating my students was experiencing the sense of achievement. I encouraged students to start at the 'Starters' level' and monitor how they progressed. Therefore, many started reading at this level. The more they read, the better they were getting and were starting to read at higher levels. This strategy worked with many students even the more advanced ones. They soon realized that they could read at a higher level and skipped some levels in order to be able to read at the right one ... The fact that they were reading at higher levels gave them a sense of progress and motivated them to challenge themselves to read more advanced stories.

In the end, it is hard to believe that those teenagers, who spent countless hours of their free time watching movies, shopping or chatting on the internet and had never read a book other than their textbooks are now reading complete novels. One of my students recently wrote to me: "At first I wasn't a big fan of reading because I had never read a complete novel or a story before".

The implementation of extensive reading programme has helped me develop as a teacher–learner myself. Not only my students' beliefs and learning habits have improved, I have also developed along with them as a teacher.

↓ IMPACT OF THE PROGRAMME ON STUDENTS' LANGUAGE DEVELOPMENT

The initial intention at the beginning of the project was to evaluate the impact of the ERP on students' language development through data gathered from students and teachers, using questionnaires and qualitative semi-structured teacher interviews at the end of the academic year. However, while monitoring the project closely, we realized that teachers needed more time to grasp the concept of the approach, make it their own, and thus implement it more successfully. As a result, we decided to extend the project into the following academic year, and follow up participating schools, enabling teachers to develop competence with the programme and hopefully share their knowledge and experience with the rest of the teaching community.

As teachers worked through the requirements of the ERP, they became increasingly confident that the approach would yield positive results for their students. The Ministry then organized a number of regular meetings where teachers were invited to discuss and reflect on their experiences and share the impact of the projects on their students; this became the basis of evaluation-setting during the second year of the programme. These teachers were also encouraged to write a brief evaluation of the project from their own perspective. Many participants provided a qualitative account of their experience and narratives describing their journey in detail. I have summarized below some of the teachers' views, based on their reflective accounts.

Motivation

Students on the ERP have become motivated to read and are usually active in classroom discussions. One teacher put it this way:

> My students have become extremely interested in reading. They are reading stories throughout the week, not only during the class.

Another teacher wrote:

> Students have started to look at the stories from another perspective, to the extent that they forget that they are actually reading and discussing in English. They are always looking forward to reading the next story.

Some teachers who had invited their students' feedback quoted their students, one of whom wrote:

> Through this program I have learned to like reading more for the purpose of "having fun" than any other reason. At the very beginning I wasn't sure about the whole thing, then when I started reading simplified stories, I found that interesting and gradually I moved to reading novels.

Another student said:

> I can't forget something our teacher told us in the first meeting "you have to enjoy while you are reading" and that [is] exactly what I feel – ENJOYING'.

Confidence in learning

Teachers also noted that some of the weaker students were developing confidence in their ability to read books suitable to their linguistic level, and were becoming more active in class discussions. According to their teachers, students in Reading Circles were getting more and more involved with their roles in the reading circles and have become more collaborative and supportive of each other. Moreover, students were also more capable of handling questions requiring greater depth of thought, and dealt with these questions with ease. As one student put it:

> At first I wasn't a big fan of reading novels and I have never read a complete novel nor a story before, but thanks to Bookworms [The Oxford Bookworms Library] it made me challenge myself and not only complete one novel, it made me read dozens of them. Not to forget to mention that the programme helped me improve my vocabulary, and writing skills.

Attitudes to learning

According to the teachers' close observations and comments, students were developing more positive attitudes towards reading classical stories. The teachers felt that the programme had empowered their students and improved their ability to integrate all the language skills. Some teachers applied the Class Reader approach with their male students, as they felt that students with limited language felt more comfortable reading this way. Most students, particularly those who were actively involved, showed great enthusiasm. As one of the second year teachers wrote:

> ... not only did the students in the Extensive Reading Programme find the stories enjoyable, other students in school who heard about the programme were interested in reading and borrowed several books from the collection of stories that the school had. I also used the stories during my substitution periods ... to encourage extensive reading among other students. The fact that stories are graded gave more motivation to students and enabled them [to] choose the suitable level. Some students were even excited to finish one level to be able to move on to the next one.

Another teacher quoted one of her students, who wrote:

> I became addicted to reading, I read every time and every where, and the best part was that I can discuss what I read with my friends. I had great times and I made great friends and I am so glad that I joined this wonderful programme and got to do all these amazing things. I mean two years ago I didn't like to read in English and now I read novels!

From studying teachers' feedback on how the project was implemented, we realized that of the three approaches introduced in schools, two seemed to be working more successfully in the Bahraini context.

In many schools, the Reading Circles approach seemed to be the one that both teachers and more competent students found most comfortable and appealing. Teachers felt that students enjoyed adopting different roles and helping each other to learn within their circles.

However, with below-average language level students, teachers felt that they could help these students better with the Class Readers approach. Because all of them read the same title at the same time, teachers were able to monitor their progress more closely as they progressed through the different levels.

From our experience, it seemed that the Class Library approach was the least successful. Our teachers were concerned that not all the students had the ability to read independently. We concluded that the Reading Circles and the Class Reader approaches are more suitable for our secondary schools.

Our ERP was launched in October 2007 as a one-year pilot project with the aim of investigating its impact on students' language development. According to information from our continuous monitoring and follow-up with schools, teachers felt that they needed more time to experience this innovative approach in order to feel convinced of its positive benefits. The Ministry agreed with this and continued to support teachers and their schools. As a result, most schools allocated additional hours to the project, and many schools are now enjoying three periods a week entirely dedicated to ER.

One of the greatest advantages of ER in Bahrain has been the development of a new teaching culture. As teachers share their success stories, more colleagues become enthusiastic and willing to implement the reading programme. (We were recently approached by the Vocational and Technical Directorate for suggestions on how to support weaker learners. When the ERP was discussed as one possibility, they became interested and requested its full implementation for Vocational and Technical students.)

Our original project started out with 15 schools. The project is now running in almost 20 schools, and gaining increased popularity among Bahraini teachers and students. Although we have not yet been able to conduct formal research on the impact of the ERP on students' language development as originally planned, our qualitative measures (observations, teachers' documents, and students' records) point to the essential role this programme has played and continues to play in fostering a culture of reading, in which students are encouraged to read at their level, their progress is monitored, and they are provided with every opportunity to enhance their language skills.

Why this works

The first important variable contributing to the positive outcome of this project is the existence of a partnership with a reputable organization. This partnership created opportunities for providing different forms of professional support to the key players in this process – the teachers. The success of any innovation largely depends on how the various stakeholders are assisted and empowered to conceptualize the value of the innovation.

The second important factor providing positive support to the project was the formation of a network of teachers involved in its implementation. The regular joint feedback meetings in which teachers voiced their concerns, shared their success stories, and helped their peers to solve their classroom problems, created a successful community of practice where teachers learned from each other and received moral and practical support on how to improve their work.

A third factor which accounted for the success of the ERP was the teachers themselves. Through my close contact with them and observation of

The Extensive Reading Programme in Bahrain

their classrooms, it became clear to me that the teachers who were most successful in the ERP were those who were passionate about the project and strongly believed that it could make a difference to their students' learning. Their enthusiasm was a driving, motivating force making the programme work for their students.

Support and motivation were the vital elements that fostered a positive learning environment. Those teachers who implemented the project successfully became role models for their colleagues, and helped to build a strong community of teacher–learners. I believe this constitutes a very effective means of sustainable development for EFL teachers. It also highlights the impact of this type of project upon teachers' personal growth.

9 Evolution of a high school Extensive Reading Programme

Daniel Stewart

↓ BACKGROUND TO THE PROGRAMME

There is no one ideal **Extensive Reading Programme** (ERP) that will work in every classroom. Every teaching situation is different, so the ideal ERP for one school will necessarily be different from that of other schools. Furthermore, school situations change over time, so programmes need to adapt to those changes. This case study illustrates some of the challenges faced by one particular school as an example of how other schools might set about creating the ideal ERP for their situation.

↓ ONE SCHOOL'S EXPERIENCE

Kaisei Academy

Kaisei is a private junior and senior high school for male students. After graduation, most of the students go on to the top universities in Japan, such as Tokyo, Keio, and Waseda. It is important to point out that while the 300 12-year-olds had to pass extremely challenging maths and science tests to enter the school, they did not take an English test. Therefore, despite attending an elite school, these students should not be considered exceptional English students.

The ERP was set up in 2002, originally with 300 third-year junior high school students. It has changed and expanded over the years and currently has 1,000 students a year from second-year junior high school to first year of high school.

↓ PREPARATION FOR THE EXTENSIVE READING PROGRAMME

The initial programme was based on ideas in *The EPER Guide to Organising Programmes of Extensive Reading* by David Hill and *Extensive Reading in the Second Language Classroom* by Richard Day and Julian Bamford. Both books contain valuable information and insights into ER for teachers starting a programme or for those wishing to improve an existing programme. Before we set up the programme, we first analysed the possible issues involved. These are listed on pages 96–101:

Evolution of a high school Extensive Reading Programme

Issue 1: cost

The first problem that needs to be solved when setting up any ERP is where to get funding for the books. There are many different ways of doing this; a number of ideas are provided in the two books referred to above. The key point is to ensure ongoing funding to replace books that get lost or damaged.

Kaisei Academy has a special fund available to teachers for classroom materials. (As an example, if a maths teacher needs a compass for every student, these can be ordered and paid for out of a special bank account.) The ERP was allocated 1,000 yen per student per year from that account for the purchase of readers. That is enough for approximately two books per student. This was regarded as a form of library fee: each student only buys two books, but the students ultimately have access to all 600 books purchased.

In addition to the cost of books, there are other minor expenses involved, such as library cards for the front of each book. For the first few years I had to purchase them myself, as the 1,000 yen library fee could only be spent on books. Once the programme was established and teachers could see the importance of the ERP, we were able to receive funding from the English department for those other expenses.

Issue 2: which books?

According to Day and Bamford, it is reasonable to start with twice as many books as there are students, but ideally there should be three or four books per student, to ensure that everyone can find readers they like at their level. Unfortunately, we only had sufficient funding to purchase two books per student per year. This meant that in the first year, before we purchased the books, all the teachers in the English Department were asked to donate any **graded readers** they no longer needed. This was a reasonable request in Japan, where teachers often receive free samples from publishers, so almost every teacher had a few books to contribute. In total we amassed about 100 books, although most of them were quite old.

Next, we consulted the lists of recommended readers at the back of *Extensive Reading in the Second Language Classroom*, compiled by David Hill of the Edinburgh Project on Extensive Reading (EPER). The lists are organized by categories such as quality of readers, and age and level of potential readers. For our secondary school students, we confined ourselves to purchasing readers with a quality rating of four or five out of five. Initially we bought only one copy of each book, so that the students would have access to as wide a variety of books as possible.

The following year (2003), we acquired the EPER list of all graded readers published since 1970. This list is probably the single most useful purchase an ER teacher could make. It is more comprehensive and up to date than the list in *Extensive Reading in the Second Language Classroom* and it ensures students get the books they need. Cost and the method of purchasing are explained on the EPER website (see 'Useful websites' on page 112).

That same year (2003), a change was instituted in the school's book-buying policy. Rather than buying 600 different books, only half the budget was spent on obtaining a range of books. The other half was spent buying class sets of the most popular books from the previous year. This was in response to a problem that had arisen in the first year – that of translation. Several books had been found with Japanese translations written over every word in the book. Clearly, at least some of the students had misunderstood the aim of the programme, so a different introductory session was planned for the second year. In the first class of the year, five minutes before the end of the lesson, every student in the class was given a copy of the same book. The teacher then read the first four or five pages to the students, while they followed in the book. The teacher read quickly, but did not rush. After four or five pages the teacher said:

> Stop. Close your book. Your homework is to finish reading this book. Don't use a dictionary. Just read it quickly and try to understand the story. Good-bye.

Almost every student immediately opened the book and continued reading as they walked back to their homeroom class. When they arrived in class the following week, they were handed a surprise test on the book. It was a very simple multiple-choice test which ensured that if they had read the book they would get full marks. After they had taken the test, the teacher pointed out that they did not have to understand every word to get a perfect score on the test. The level of understanding they needed for each book they read was to understand the general meaning of the story and not the meaning of every single word. This innovative system of introducing ER worked extremely well, and students continued to be tested on the first book they read each year until 2006, when the tests for every book were posted on a website. Further discussion of this is given in the section 'Keeping track of students' reading' below.

More recently the school has given up buying single copies of readers. At least five or six copies of each book are purchased at one time so as to promote a community of readers.

Try this ☞ **Encourage group activities with books**

Here are a few possible activities, when five or six students can all sign out copies of the same book:

- suggest skits and role-plays during class time: each member of a group takes a copy of the book home to read. Later, in class, the students in each group get together and write a play script to be performed
- ask the students to change the story in some way, such as changing the main character from a man to a woman, the location from New York to New Delhi, or the time from 2005 to 1905. Each student then rewrites part of the story in a different way. In the next class, the students exchange their work and read it. This gives them a chance to use the language they are learning. It is much easier to rewrite something than to create something entirely original. It also gives the students a feeling of success, as their friends are really interested in reading what they have written.

Evolution of a high school Extensive Reading Programme

 *Getting it right*

Keep the collection attractive

It is interesting to note that virtually none of the original 100 donated books remain in the school collection. They were quite old to begin with; when they started to fall apart, they were removed from the collection. We made it clear to teachers that they must be willing to throw or give away damaged books, because if students see damaged books in the collection, they are likely to feel that it is acceptable to mistreat books. Students are also much more likely to be drawn to attractive books, so damaged ones should be avoided where possible.

Issue 3: dictionaries

The ERP at Kaisei started out in 2002 with a strict 'no dictionary' rule, since Day and Bamford had pointed out that this rule is a useful way of differentiating ER from Intensive Reading (IR). The students were willing to follow the rule, so it remained in place until a new teacher arrived at the school and questioned the validity of the policy. The available research on dictionary use in ER was reviewed and it was found that there was not enough empirical evidence to show whether students should be allowed to use dictionaries or not.

I decided to research this issue as the topic of my MA dissertation. In this study, 286 students took a standardized pre-ERP test and then worked with ER for eight months. Students in my study were allowed to use dictionaries, but were required to keep track of how often they used them. All students in the study improved their scores on the standardized post-ERP test, but some improved more than others. Among the light readers (the 95 students who read fewer than 18,300 words), those who occasionally used dictionaries improved more than those who never used a dictionary or those who used a dictionary more often. Meanwhile the 95 medium readers (18,300–31,199 words) who never used a dictionary improved more than medium readers who did use a dictionary. Finally for the 96 relatively heavy readers who read more than 31,199 words, dictionary use did not seem to be a factor.

Therefore the current dictionary policy was updated to allow students to use dictionaries in their ER, but with the stated proviso that they try to use them less and less, until they no longer needed them at all.

Issue 4: getting the books to the students

Originally the graded readers were to have been stored in the school library, where the students could sign them out at any time, but that turned out to be impossible because the library has its own policies about buying books. Instead the teachers themselves physically carried the books to the classroom where the reading classes were held.

✓ *Getting it right*

Locate suitable book storage

In the first year it was still possible to carry the graded readers to the classroom, because at least 300 of the 700 were always signed out. However, when an additional 600 books were purchased the following year, it would have been necessary to carry 1,000 books to the classroom every day. Clearly this was not going to work. Eventually, the readers were stored in some empty lockers near the classroom. Every day, the teachers would then have to spread out the boxes of books across the empty desks at the back of the classroom. Unfortunately, the books had to be removed after each class, as the same classroom was also used for other subjects. It soon became clear that a better solution was needed – and this was to purchase one of the Brodart Library Supply Company's book carts (see illustration below). Now the books are kept on the cart and rolled into the classroom when needed. Problem solved.

FIGURE 9.1   *Example of a graded reader mobile book cart*

Interestingly, the original plan (to store the readers in the school library) has now been realized to some extent. As a result of the success of the reading programme, the school librarians approached the ERP Director asking for recommendations for English books for the library. The result was that students can now borrow books in class or from the library.

Evolution of a high school Extensive Reading Programme

Issue 5: signing out books

The standard system for signing books out, using a card at the front of each book, was used for the first few years. However, once there were thousands of books in the system, cards were lost or ended up in the wrong book. This was particularly common when there were several copies of the same book; for example, the card for copy two might appear in the sleeve of copy 12. Books without the correct card had to be removed from the trolley and it was often the most popular books that were without cards. A professional library sign-out system was considered, but the $10,000 cost for the system was beyond the programme's budget.

Instead a custom-made barcode system was created to keep track of the books. The FileMaker Pro database program was already being used to keep track of the ERP books, so all that was needed was a portable barcode reader, a barcode font, and some address labels. Barcodes were printed on the address labels and then stuck on each book. A list of students was also prepared with their student numbers printed in a barcode font. A barcode reader called the Flic by Microvision was then used to get the information from the barcodes into the computer. By using a portable barcode reader, it is not necessary to carry a laptop computer to class.

Here is how the system works:

- A student selects a book and brings it to the teacher.
- The teacher uses the barcode reader to read the barcode on the back of the book.
- The teacher then reads in the barcode beside the student's name – their student number. That becomes the current location of the book.
- When the teacher returns to the teachers' room, the barcode reader is plugged in to the computer and the current location of the book is recorded in the database program.
- When the book is returned to the teacher, the teacher uses the barcode reader to change the current location back to library.

This system worked well for two years until the button on the Flic began to stick. Microvision has since replaced the Flic with an updated version called the ROV.

 *Getting it right*

Use a barcode tracking system

By using a barcode reader instead of the old card-based system, more of the books were available for the students and the database made it possible to find the current location of any book. This proved very useful when students needed several copies of the same book for a play. The location of every copy of a title could be found immediately. With the old card-based system, finding that information used to take a considerable amount of time.

Issue 6: keeping track of students' reading

Most ERPs require students to keep track of what they have read. The programme at Kaisei is no exception. From 2002 to 2005, a version of the chart shown below was used. In the 'Quality' column students had to rank the book on a scale of one to five and circle the correct number of stars, five stars being the best. The other columns are self-explanatory.

Books I Have Read

Name: .... **Student Number:** ....

Book Name	Level	Quality	# of words	Total # of words	# of times a dictionary was used
1		★ ★ ★ ★ ★			
2		★ ★ ★ ★ ★			
3		★ ★ ★ ★ ★			

FIGURE 9.2　*An example of a student reading record chart*

The original chart did not include the last column on dictionary use. It was added when that issue was being researched. The chart was effective because the students could see the rise in their reading level and total number of words read. However, there were two problems with this system:

First, it did not show if the student had really read the book. Fortunately, in our particular ERP, the books students read for homework were also used in class, so it was clear whether they had read the books or not.

Try this ☞ **Get students to 'promote' a reader**

One task in class might be for students to convince their partners to read a certain book. It would be immediately obvious to you if a student had not read their homework book and it inspires students to read what their friends have just read.

Second, the data generated by the chart was under-utilized. There was a mass of information a teacher could use to help students, but no way of accessing it other than reading 300 charts to look for patterns.

The solution was to create a website combining this chart with the simple paper tests that had been used on the second day of class since 2003. This website is known as Booktests. All 300 students in the ERP have been using the Booktests website since April 2006. The site is continually upgraded to make it more useful for the students and teachers who use it. Thomas Robb has also created a website based on the simple test idea. This is explained in detail in Chapter 10 (see pages 106–8) so only the main points of the site being used by Kaisei students will be discussed here.

Try this ☞ **Ensure your students have read their homework reader**

When your students have finished reading a book, get them to log in to the Booktests website, using a secret username and password. They get five minutes to complete a very simple test on the book. If they have read the book, they are likely to get a perfect score, but it would be very difficult for them to get even a pass score if they had not read the book!

Note: You, as a teacher, are welcome to use the Booktests website free on condition that you allow me to use the anonymous data it generates for my research.

In the case of Kaisei, I myself wrote every test to ensure consistency of quality and to be sure that no one else has a copy of the tests. The security of the tests is vital to my research, as I propose to use the data for doctoral research in the future. Other teachers do use the Booktests website, but they do not have access to my tests. The teachers who use it are sent a report on their students by email. For example, if teacher X is teaching Class 2 on Tuesday at 9:00 a.m., the website automatically generates data for him on Class 2 at 7:00 a.m. on Tuesday and sends him an Excel file email like the one below.

A	B	C	D	E	F	G
User name	Quiz #s	Quiz Avg.	Level Avg.	Dict Avg.	Rating Avg.	Words Read
61jackal	7	4	2.7	2	7	24723
61jackrabbit	7	3	2.4	0	5.4	21100
61jay	13	4.7	2.4	6.8	9.5	46672
61kangaroo	17	3.1	2.4	6.4	6.6	57060

FIGURE 9.3   *An example of a student test report*

In essence, the website allows teachers to make effective use of the data collected on the paper graph. For example, at this point in the year students are supposed to have read seven books. The teacher can quickly scan down the chart and see which students he needs to discuss his concerns with. Here, 61jackrabbit and 61kangaroo both have quite low average scores on their five-point quizzes. He might:

- talk to both these students about the books they are choosing, on account of their low rating scores
- get them to ask their friends what books they have enjoyed
- suggest they read a few level 2 books instead of level 3, so that they can understand them more easily.

Also note it would be useful to give 61jay some pointers on how to guess meaning from context instead of using his dictionary so often.

↓ THE EXPANDING PROGRAMME

While all the issues outlined above were being dealt with, the situation at Kaisei was slowly changing. Teachers outside the ERP started noticing the programme and became more supportive. The clearest example of this was the case of the junior high second-year teachers. The ERP had always involved the third-year students and their native-English speaking teachers. Four years ago a Japanese teacher agreed to cancel his English grammar classes for his second-year students for the first month of the year. Instead he took them to the library where they read graded readers in a

Sustained Silent Reading (SSR) situation. This new practice was seen as useful by the teachers and enjoyable by the students, so it has been continued in the last three years by all teachers of second-year students. It seems that once a system is established and regarded as useful, others are willing to get involved.

At Kaisei, there are only eight weeks of classes in the third term of the first year of high school. Unfortunately, every year several classes have to be cancelled because of entrance exams. While six class periods is not enough to teach new ER material, it has been found that SSR is an effective complement to ER. The school has a substantial collection of books written for native speakers, from very simple books such as the Oxford Project X series, to Harry Potter. Students are able to sit and read any books they like, and they find this is a very satisfying way to end the year.

Try this ☞ **Encourage group activities with books**

Put the students in groups of six and have all of them secretly pick one scene from the book they are all currently reading and draw a picture of it at home. It must not be a copy of a picture that is already in the book. Then in the next class, the other five students look at the picture and race to find that scene in their books. This gets the artistic students interested in the reading, and the student who knows the book best usually wins the race. Finally, everyone gets practice at skimming.

Try this ☞ **Discuss reading and other matters individually**

Students are often reluctant to voice their concerns publicly in front of their peers. One way round this would be to call your students up one at a time while the rest are engaged in SSR, to chat about the books they are reading, or anything else they would like to talk about.

Earlier I mentioned that there are 300 students in each grade, but an additional 100 students join the school in the fourth grade. These new 15-year-olds have to take an English test to enter the school, so their English level is generally high. Interestingly their listening skills range from weak to native-like. The students who have already studied at Kaisei for three years generally have good listening skills, since they were required to do a considerable amount of listening practice for homework in junior high school. Helping the new students whose listening skills are weak to catch up without boring the native-like listeners was a problem solved by introducing Extensive Listening homework (see 'Try this' below).

Try this ☞ **Suggest listening practice for all students**

Many graded readers come with an accompanying CD. Some weak readers are better at learning through listening. Encourage weak readers to take home a graded reader and listen to the CD as they read. You might find they do better that way. For all students, using the CD not only improves their listening, but gives them a chance to be exposed to English spoken in a variety of different accents.

An additional advantage to this as a listening skills activity is that by listening to the recording, students are also exposed to spoken English. For those who learn better by listening than reading, this provides and extra chance to improve.

Evolution of a high school Extensive Reading Programme

Evolution of a high school Extensive Reading Programme

Why this works

The ERP at Kaisei has evolved since 2002 and is expected to continue doing so. Initially the project was based on ideas found in textbooks, but it was later modified to suit the needs of the school. As the school changed over time, the programme has changed as well. The most important discovery we made was that once a programme is established and has demonstrably worthwhile, positive results, more and more teachers and others are willing to get involved. It is hoped that readers of this book will use this example to create the ideal ERP for their own schools.

References

Day, R. R. and J. Bamford. 1998. *Extensive Reading in the Second Language Classroom*. Cambridge: Cambridge University Press.

Hill, D. R. 1992. *The EPER guide to organising programmes of extensive reading*. Edinburgh: Institute for Applied Language Studies, University of Edinburgh.

10 A digital solution for Extensive Reading

Thomas Robb

Although many teachers now understand the value of **Extensive Reading** (ER), an appreciation of its benefits does not often translate into actual implementation. In any educational establishment, there are some formidable obstacles to be overcome for an Extensive Reading Programme (ERP) to be effective. If any one element is missing, ER simply does not work. The most serious obstacles and problems are:

- **budget:** obtaining a sufficient number of books
- **management:** managing book loans to ensure that books are returned
- **motivation:** getting the students to read the books
- **assessment:** making sure that students have read what they claim to have read.

Other chapters in this book contain suggestions for obtaining and managing books. What is unique about the ERP at Kyoto Sangyo University (KSU) is our approach to motivating and assessing the students (the last two items listed above). Simply put, the students are given a reading requirement for the term and they have to prove that they have read the books by answering easy quizzes on their computers, thus keeping track (for their own and their teachers' benefit) of how much they have read during the term.

Students are often reluctant to do homework if they suspect or know their work will not be seen or assessed by their teacher. If they are not held accountable for the ER they are expected to do, they will be tempted to spend that time working on some other course material, where the additional work would be evaluated by their instructor and thus improve their grade in that subject.

A single teacher implementing ER might be able to assess students' reading by having them write book reports, or perhaps by having them deliver oral reports in class. But there is a limit to how much class time can be spent on work which is supposed to have been done outside the classroom. In addition, written reports create an even heavier workload for the already over-taxed teacher. Furthermore, instructors who are teaching part time are usually not in a position to implement ER, nor can they be asked to review a new batch of written reports every week.

Fortunately, a computerized solution such as the Moodle Reader module neatly solves these problems. It allows the students to read books at their own pace, and to answer a short quiz (which they can usually complete in 3–4 minutes) in order to prove that they have read the book. The questions are drawn from a question bank, which makes it difficult for students to cheat. The quizzes can be downloaded from any Internet-connected computer, so there is no need for computers to be used within the school. In fact, although KSU has plenty of computers on campus for student use, the most popular time to take quizzes is between midnight and one in the morning!

The English Department at KSU has been using ER with first-year students for over 20 years. Since **graded readers** designed for non-native speakers were not generally available at that time, we started with 'Youth Literature', books popular with native speaking pre-teens and teenagers. Some years later, when we extended ER to our second-year students, we made a massive investment in The Oxford Bookworms Library graded readers.

In order to track their reading, we initially required written summaries from the students, but these were so tedious for the students to write and for the teachers to read, that about 10 years ago we started using a programme popular with schools in the USA and Canada, called 'Accelerated Reader' (AR) which offers pre-made quizzes for over 25,000 book titles. Unfortunately, this programme did not offer any pre-made tests for graded readers at all, so our staff had to read each Bookworm title and prepare a quiz for it. But this posed a serious problem: the system only allowed for a maximum of 100 'teacher-made' quizzes. Furthermore, all students received the same 10 questions, always presented in the same order, so gradually 'cheat sheets' began to circulate, thus defeating the purpose of using the programme. We were forced to invigilate the students' quiz-taking by restricting the test-taking time to the noon hour, with one teacher present every day.

We used the AR system for a number of years, but as we gradually shifted towards graded readers, we ran up against the teacher-made quiz limit. The need for a better system, free of these defects, gave birth to the Moodle Reader.

Moodle Reader

I was already using Moodle – a popular, free, open-source course management system which is relatively easy to modify and add special functions to. It was therefore the natural choice for developing a special quiz-tracking programme. The Moodle quiz module was already able to produce suitable quizzes for the students, but what was needed was a system that could:

- pace the students' quiz taking, so that they did not attempt to fulfil their reading requirement in the last few days or weeks of the term
- provide a clear, understandable record of students' progress
- require no invigilation by teachers during student quiz-taking
- control the quizzes students took to ensure they didn't try to fulfil their requirement with over-easy material, nor attempt a book that was so difficult that they would be forced to revert to an intensive, word-by-word approach.

Figure 10.1 below displays the interface we came up with, using an actual student's record (name changed) for the example. The top of the screen shows the cover of each book for which the quiz was successfully passed. This is followed by a book-by-book listing showing how many words the student has read and how many points have been gathered. The progress bar gives a graphic example of the total number of words read.

KSU has defined the module settings so that students can take a few quizzes either one level below or one level above their current level. This is explained in the fine print on the screen. Finally, in this example, two days have passed since the student last took a quiz, so he can now attempt another one. (As with all of the other settings, the teachers/administrators can set these to suit their own programme.)

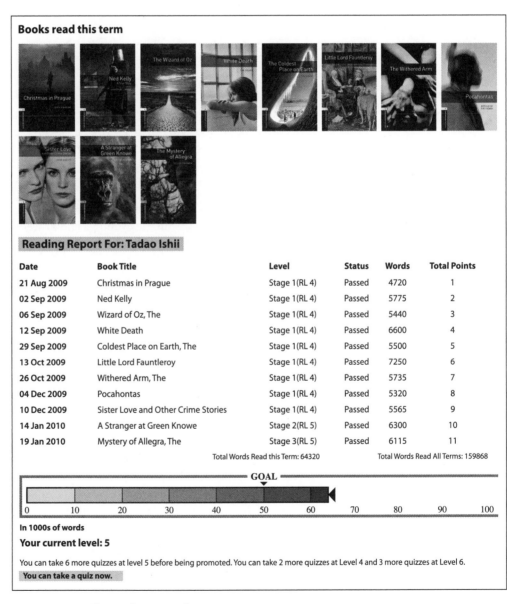

Books read this term

Reading Report For: Tadao Ishii

Date	Book Title	Level	Status	Words	Total Points
21 Aug 2009	Christmas in Prague	Stage 1(RL 4)	Passed	4720	1
02 Sep 2009	Ned Kelly	Stage 1(RL 4)	Passed	5775	2
06 Sep 2009	Wizard of Oz, The	Stage 1(RL 4)	Passed	5440	3
12 Sep 2009	White Death	Stage 1(RL 4)	Passed	6600	4
29 Sep 2009	Coldest Place on Earth, The	Stage 1(RL 4)	Passed	5500	5
13 Oct 2009	Little Lord Fauntleroy	Stage 1(RL 4)	Passed	7250	6
26 Oct 2009	Withered Arm, The	Stage 1(RL 4)	Passed	5735	7
04 Dec 2009	Pocahontas	Stage 1(RL 4)	Passed	5320	8
10 Dec 2009	Sister Love and Other Crime Stories	Stage 1(RL 4)	Passed	5565	9
14 Jan 2010	A Stranger at Green Knowe	Stage 2(RL 5)	Passed	6300	10
19 Jan 2010	Mystery of Allegra, The	Stage 3(RL 5)	Passed	6115	11

Total Words Read this Term: 64320   Total Words Read All Terms: 159868

GOAL

| 0 | 10 | 20 | 30 | 40 | 50 | 60 | 70 | 80 | 90 | 100 |

In 1000s of words

Your current level: 5

You can take 6 more quizzes at level 5 before being promoted. You can take 2 more quizzes at Level 4 and 3 more quizzes at Level 6.

You can take a quiz now.

FIGURE 10.1   *The student record*

A digital solution for Extensive Reading

Figure 10.2 shows the quiz selection screen. Students only see quizzes for those books that they are currently eligible to take quizzes on.

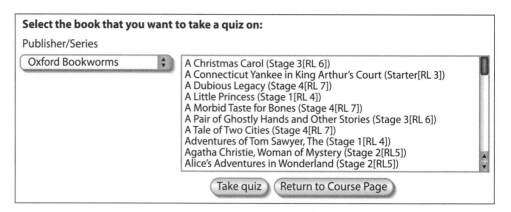

Select the book that you want to take a quiz on:

Publisher/Series

Oxford Bookworms

A Christmas Carol (Stage 3[RL 6])
A Connecticut Yankee in King Arthur's Court (Starter[RL 3])
A Dubious Legacy (Stage 4[RL 7])
A Little Princess (Stage 1[RL 4])
A Morbid Taste for Bones (Stage 4[RL 7])
A Pair of Ghostly Hands and Other Stories (Stage 3[RL 6])
A Tale of Two Cities (Stage 4[RL 7])
Adventures of Tom Sawyer, The (Stage 1[RL 4])
Agatha Christie, Woman of Mystery (Stage 2[RL5])
Alice's Adventures in Wonderland (Stage 2[RL5])

Take quiz   Return to Course Page

FIGURE 10.2   *The quiz selection screen*

The Moodle Reader was implemented in April 2008 with all of the first year English majors and International Relations majors in the Faculty of Foreign Languages, with a total of 210 students participating. They were required to read eight books in the first term (April–July) and twelve books in the second term (September–January). Students were told that they would lose half a mark of their final evaluation (out of 100) for each book not read, and gain half a mark for each book read over the target amount.

We found that the programme worked. Surprisingly, students took most of their quizzes at home in the evenings and at weekends (something that had not been an option under the old system).

Expansion from English majors to general education

At KSU, I am not only a member of the English Department, but also Chair of the General Education English Programme, which supervises the English language instruction for all other sections of the university, with the exception of the Faculty of International Culture, which has its own curriculum and teachers. In November of 2008, we took a bold step and decided to extend the ERP to all first-year English classes in the university. This amounted to a total of around 2,300 students in 140 classes, each of which met twice a week for 90 minutes.

There are 60 teachers involved in teaching these courses, 11 full-time teachers who quickly embraced the concept, but the rest were part-time teachers who mostly had never heard of ER, much less conducted classes in it. Fortunately, we were in a position to do the unthinkable: require the students to read, but without using the individual teachers as intermediaries. Our plan was simple. We decided to:

- inform the teachers that ER would be added to the curriculum the following year, and explain the basic concept to them
- ask them to include information about the ER requirement in their course descriptions, using a set text we provided to them

- supply all the teachers with handouts explaining in Japanese the purpose of ER, the requirement (five books per student per term), where to borrow books (the library reserve book section), the URL for the quizzes, the basic procedure and rules for taking the quizzes, and how their reading would be evaluated
- provide each teacher with a pre-prepared Excel spreadsheet at the end of the term showing how many marks to add or subtract from each student's grade.

While teachers were free to conduct in-class activities to promote ER, we did not expect the instructors to deal with it in class unless they wanted to. Teachers could, if they wished, review the current status of their students on the Moodle Reader website at any time and, on an optional basis, counsel students who were under-achieving.

There were inevitably a few hitches in the execution of the programme – such as teachers who failed to hand out the information to the students; a shortage of books in the library for some levels; students who opened a quiz and then closed it, expecting to be able to open it a second time, and so on – but by and large, most of the students read at least some books. In all, 28,156 quizzes were taken by 2,260 students, for an average of 12.5 books per student. As a result, the class of 2009 showed a significant improvement over the class of 2008 in their reading scores on our final examination, despite the fact that both groups were equivalent in ability at the beginning of the year, according to our placement test data. Both years used nearly identical teaching material and methodology in the classroom, with essentially the same cohort of teachers. The only variable that can explain the improvement in their reading scores is the ER experience.

Try this ☞　**Experiment with the Moodle Reader in your own curriculum**

A significant merit of the Moodle Reader is that, assuming graded readers can be placed in the hands of the students, you can easily implement it in your own curriculum. Rather than having a few enthusiastic teachers who carry out ER while the rest continue to teach in the traditional way, implementation of the Moodle Reader allows you or the administration of the school to say, quite simply: 'Everyone will do ER next year.'

The Moodle Reader module is available on the Internet (see 'Useful websites' on page 112) and is free of charge for use by any established educational institution. Each school is given a course with their own school colours and logo and can enrol their students in it, divided into class units to facilitate tracking the students. The module has quizzes available on approximately 900 graded reader titles, including all The Oxford Bookworms Library, from Starter level to level 6. Work to add the Dominoes series is now in progress.

Why this works

The KSU experience shows that an ERP can be administered effectively at the school level, without the individual teacher having to 'buy in' to the pedagogy. Naturally, enthusiastic teachers who explain the merits of ER

A digital solution for Extensive Reading

to their students, act as role models by reading themselves, and carry on activities in the class to allow students to share their reading experiences with each other will be more effective. Nevertheless, even if there are teachers who merely inform their students of the reading requirement outside of class, and only incorporate the students' Extensive Reading grade into the final evaluation as dictated by the administration, the system still affords students extended contact with English outside the classroom, raising their ability to cope with long English texts and to become more familiar with the syntax, lexis, and **collocations** of the English language.

11

A class library project in Italy

Nina Prentice

↓ BACKGROUND TO THE PROJECT

Read On! is an Italy-wide class library project inaugurated in 2011. Promoting inclusive, collaborative, creative, and student-centred learning, it trains teachers to use a lively selection of age-appropriate, graded readers from Oxford University Press to build an active classroom community. Students become protagonists. They manage the libraries, choose what to read, how to respond, and then peer-review their efforts. Teachers collaborate: reading alongside their students, sharing conversations about books, and facilitating student responses to reading.

Recent international surveys rank Italy in last place in literacy (OECD 2013) and penultimate in Europe in English proficiency (EF: EPI 2014). There is also a sharp north-south divide in literacy and English language skills, with southern Italian regions weakest in both competences (ISTAT 2014).

To address these problems, the Italian Ministry of Education has launched numerous initiatives to improve outcomes for students: promoting e-textbooks, digitizing classrooms, and retraining teachers. Other strands of Italian educational reform include introducing Content and Language Integrated Learning (**CLIL**) into the final year of some secondary schools, adopting CLIL approaches in lower secondary classes and legislating for inclusion for students with Special Educational Needs (**SEN**). Despite these efforts, Italian students are not acquiring the 21st-century skills necessary for the workplace such as collaboration, problem solving, creativity, life-long learning, and mobility.

Many Italian teachers of English still rely heavily on content-based, grammar translation approaches. Frequent testing confines students' learning to the test topics rather than promoting effective communication in English. Poor outcomes in school often oblige parents to pay for extra tuition or trips abroad to improve their children's level of English and to acquire internationally recognized language certifications.

↓ WHY CHOOSE *READ ON!*?

Students who read extensively acquire skills and competences which help to bypass ineffectual teaching and poor use of time or resources in school. It also gives teachers fresh input and innovative approaches to teaching to help them change and grow as educators. Most importantly, it gives everyone a chance to learn, whatever their circumstances or ability.

A class library project in Italy

Read On! has the following six main objectives.

- **Offering students the opportunity to become motivated autonomous learners:** Most Italians are not readers and the dislike of reading starts in school where it's a compulsory and heavily evaluated activity involving difficult texts chosen by teachers or by textbook authors. Unsurprisingly, students associate reading with obligation, difficulty, and testing. Instead, a *Read On!* class library offers a varied and level-appropriate choice of texts and promotes the idea that reading for pleasure can be a powerful driver of learning. Choice is motivating and students discover that they can learn painlessly without drills, comprehension exercises, or formal evaluation. Encouraged to respond as they wish to their reading, students learn to communicate, collaborate, and problem-solve creatively.

- **Promoting critical reading and thinking skills for the 21st century:** Decoding text is only the first step on the long road to becoming an effective reader. Genuine critical literacy involves dedicated practice and traditional reading at school rarely supplies it. By contrast, access to a *Read On!* library allows students to appreciate the pleasures of reading through choice, discussion, and research interests. As they become more confident, learners' use of grammar, structures, and vocabulary become fluent. Learners then have more mental capacity to engage in higher levels of critical literacy: the ability to use, talk, and think about text.

- **Developing students' and teachers' awareness of digital citizenship and academic responsibility:** Responses to the class library often involve researching both online and offline to produce a range of products – traditional and digital. Italian students and their teachers have relatively little awareness of effective web search skills, the rules of copyright or digital responsibility. The project educates students and teachers to become more mindful of these issues. All competitions and submissions require students to acknowledge sources, cite correctly, and avoid plagiarism and illegal downloads.

- **Promoting inclusion:** In recent years the Italian Ministry of Education has legislated extensively to promote inclusion, focussing on SEN. Many parts of the country have growing immigrant populations with children learning English as an additional language in school. Despite the legislation, there is little support for teachers tackling these issues. A graded class library provides teacher training and differentiated resources for students in any classroom, whatever their needs or abilities. Reading for pleasure gives every child the opportunity to learn without fear of failure.

- **Supporting effective CLIL teaching:** The Italian Ministry of Education has adopted CLIL methodology but many teachers involved in the initiative are struggling to implement it successfully. The *Read On!* project became involved in CLIL at the Ministry's request and has designed an extensive reading scheme with a focus on English skills and digital skills for cross-curricular learning. Rather than simply reading CLIL subject-focussed textbooks, students are encouraged to link whatever text they may be reading for pleasure from their class library to their CLIL subject, follow up with web-based research and then present the link to their fellow students or post online to the larger CLIL community.

- **Changing teachers' perceptions of their role in the 21st-century classroom:** *Read On!* focuses on quality training to give teachers the skills to get students reading and learning autonomously. The programme recruits selectively, only issuing libraries to those teachers who commit to the core principles of extensive reading (e.g. choice, autonomy, and freedom from formal evaluations). It then sustains students both online and offline to ensure they feel part of the *Read On!* 'family'. In a country where training tends to be top-down and theoretical, the project provides practical seminars, online support, and student-focussed events to motivate and refresh teachers' commitment to extensive reading and its potential in the classroom.

↓ SETTING UP THE PROJECT

Libraries

Each level of schooling has its own selection of age-appropriate, graded readers from Oxford University Press which, along with a storage suitcase, can be purchased as a package with its own code or ISBN. There are three different libraries: primary, lower secondary, and upper secondary. Each library contains approximately ninety books chosen by popularity and the availability of an audio CD – an important resource for Italian readers.

Storage

Each library is stored in a lockable trolley suitcase. This solution resolves the problem of security for the books because teachers or students can easily move the trolley from a safe storage area to the classroom and back.

Funding

The *Read On!* project is dedicated to providing opportunities for disadvantaged children with less access to high-quality teaching and educational initiatives, particularly in southern regions. On their behalf, the programme sought support from British companies working in Italy and they provided the initial funding for libraries. More recently, Italian companies have joined the sponsorship scheme for the programme. Since *Read On!* became an accepted methodology, teachers and schools have found it easier to raise funds to finance the libraries from public sources, school administrations or parents.

Training

Teachers' enthusiasm for and commitment to an extensive reading approach are vital for the successful delivery of the programme. *Read On!* trainers continue to refine and adapt the training package to include best practice emerging from the classroom. Regular sessions, the *Read On!* website, and online support allow both trainees and *Read On!* 'veterans' to share success stories, strategies, and concerns.

Guidelines

All teachers joining the project are asked to respect the following guidelines.

Committing to the methodology

Only those teachers who are prepared to commit to the principles of extensive reading are invited to join the programme. Libraries are issued after teachers have attended training and participants are supported as long as they continue to work with the project.

The library belongs to one class for one academic year

For the following important reasons, libraries are never shared with more than one class over a twelve-month period.

- **Borrowing:** When libraries are divided between classes, the borrowing system breaks down and students read significantly fewer books because of lack of choice.
- **Focus:** Knowing that the library is available to their class for only one year prompts students to take maximum advantage of this opportunity 'to read their way to better English'.
- **Ownership:** Students take great pride in having a library available exclusively in their classroom. If the library is shared with more than one group, students lose interest – blaming other classes for reducing the availability of books or for not looking after them properly.
- **'Passing the torch' – the library as a living legacy:** After reading extensively for a year, students hand over the library to their successors in a public ceremony. The veteran class is encouraged to add new books to the original selection as a thank-you for the loan and to update the library with favourite books and resource packs for the upcoming class.

Choice is at the heart of the project

Giving learners the opportunity to decide what to read, how to respond, and how to present their research motivates and stimulates genuine learning and promotes creativity and autonomy.

No formal testing or other traditional evaluations of reading

If we really want students to learn to read for pleasure, then testing, book reports, and comprehension exercises have no place on an extensive reading programme.

Promoting student responsibility and autonomy

Read On! students learn to:

- **manage their libraries independently** by electing librarians, deciding how their borrowing system will work, ensuring that the library is available in every English lesson, and dealing with lost or stolen books.

- **track their reading with reading passports** in primary and **reading logs** in secondary. These resources, available on the *Read On!* website, help students to continue reading throughout the academic year. Having regular, achievable goals encourages learners to read up to a million words (approximately 2–2.5 books per week) in that year.
- **work collaboratively** by responding to their reading in groups and working on projects in teams. Developing collaborative skills motivates but also prepares students to face the challenges of the 21st-century workplace where teamwork is the norm.
- **research critically**. *Read On!* students not only learn how to search effectively both online and offline for relevant information, they also develop their ability to evaluate and synthesize their findings to present to the class or the wider community.
- **respond creatively** by producing their own artwork, craft, drama, text, video, and music prompted by their reading experiences. Students are encouraged to avoid 'ready-made' platforms and, instead, to learn how to create their own sound, image, and graphics.
- **exercise digital and academic responsibility** when downloading image, sound, or text from the internet. Avoid all acts of plagiarism including 'cutting and pasting' and failing to acknowledge and cite sources correctly.
- **practice self- and peer-assessment** as opposed to being subject to the teacher-led evaluative practices which normally occur in Italian language classrooms (e.g. high-stakes testing, exhaustive written book reports and comprehension exercises). Students instead agree on their own assessment criteria for extensive reading activities and then carry out self- or peer- assessment of their work within these frameworks.

Celebrating success

Student effort and achievement are regularly rewarded and celebrated in the classroom. The *Read On!* website offers certificates for all kinds of achievement, and for all kinds of learners. The programme encourages teachers to see success not simply in terms of tests and grades. Instead, they learn to recognize that effort, creativity, and targets reached by all members of the class, whatever their ability, are key outcomes for long-term learning and success.

No orphan libraries

As long as teachers are on the programme, the library remains their property, available for a new class to use every new academic year. If, for whatever reason, a teacher wishes to leave the project, they should make arrangements to ensure that the library goes to another trained and committed teacher within the school or in the area. The library must continue working with new classes, year on year.

A class library project in Italy

The *Read On!* website (www.oup.com/elt/readon) provides a regularly updated platform presenting teacher resources, student output, ideas, and good practice. Teachers and students visit the site to get inspiration to stimulate reading, manage libraries, and produce good-quality responses to reading. Resources available include the following.

- **Teacher-training packs:** As well as receiving training materials when they join the programme, teachers can download these resources as needed from the website.
- **Primary and secondary teacher-training films:** These show how *Read On!* can work successfully in the classroom with different age groups. Separate episodes show teachers how to introduce the library to students, talk about books, exploit the audio CDs, create on-the-spot activities, and use drama as well as other successful approaches.
- **Resources for librarians:** Over the years, student librarians have shared the strategies they have used to manage their libraries effectively. The resources range from simple borrowing logs to complex spreadsheets tracking students' reading, favourite books, and genres over the year by individual, sex, or age.
- **Primary reading passports and secondary logs:** The point of extensive reading is to get students 'hooked on books'. *Read On!* students are challenged to read the whole library in the course of the year. The primary passport and secondary logs divide this reading challenge into manageable targets and allow students to track progress, record likes or dislikes, and celebrate achievement.
- **Downloadable certificates:** These are awarded to students to celebrate achievements and outstanding effort. Teachers are encouraged to reward student success of all kinds and not see achievement only in terms of conventional academic progress and memory skills.
- **Web-search cards:** These have been developed from cross-curricular work with CLIL and offer themed challenges based on different selections of books in the *Read On!* library. Students are encouraged to read the books and then research particular areas of interest both online and offline. Working collaboratively, students present findings to the class in their choice of media with the express aim of developing English communication skills, whatever the subject.
- **Academic responsibility and digital citizenship:** Downloadable resources linked to the research activities teach students (and teachers) to respect copyright, cite correctly, and never download music, images, or video illegally.
- **Anniversary activities:** Both students and teachers are encouraged to celebrate key anniversaries, for example, the bicentenary of the publication of *Pride and Prejudice* produced some outstanding videos. To commemorate the start of the First World War, there is a dedicated web-search card, and a Milan EXPO 2015 card explores the EXPO theme: *Feeding the Planet, Energy for Life*.
- **Innovative responses to reading:** The website also publishes examples of student responses to reading. The range is extraordinary and includes video, dressmaking, puppets, and baking!

In addition the online resources offered by the *Read On!* project, other successful strategies and important features include the following.

Inclusion

Read On! is dedicated to offering all learners, whatever their circumstances or abilities, the opportunity to make progress in English through extensive reading and associated activities. Teachers ask open questions rather than putting students on the spot. Group activities promoting collaboration and the sharing of students' skills are encouraged. Alternative approaches using audio CDs, drama and illustration aim to give everyone in class a chance to succeed and be valued. Effort is celebrated and rewarded.

CLIL

In 2011, the Italian Ministry of Education commissioned *Read On!* for *e*CLIL. Paired subject-specialist teachers and English-teaching colleagues started working together in CLIL teams to create cross-curricular learning opportunities. The libraries have proved invaluable for this collaboration by providing a wide variety of differentiated resources that students have been able to use as starting points for a comprehensive range of subject-specific research and presentations. Students have read the Charles Dickens stories and then researched the Industrial Revolution and labour legislation. Others have made thoughtful connections with texts in the library and scientific and mathematical topics. For example, students used *Sherlock Holmes and the Sport of Kings* to look at betting and probability or *The Elephant Man* to research genetically inherited disease, and then employed different digital media to present findings. CLIL strategies are now a part of the mainstream project and the methodology is being practised from primary through to secondary. Additionally, teachers have also found that reading the texts in the libraries alongside the class has not only refreshed their English but also given them real insight into their students as individuals.

End-of-year festivals

Many *Read On!* classes have arranged a festival to celebrate their work and the reading achievements of the year. These can be simple school events, citywide, or even regional occasions. Participating students set up stands to showcase what they have done, which can include artefacts of all kinds from new designs for covers, themed games, and recycled gadgets to sophisticated digital productions. Parents, local authorities, sponsors, and members of the school community visit the stands and talk to students about their reading and responses to the books they have enjoyed. Also on these occasions, downloadable certificates are awarded for effort, creativity, and number of books read. Students and teachers appreciate the opportunity to showcase what they have done during the year and the festival helps promote the idea that books are the best teachers.

Since its launch in 2011, teachers have been overwhelmingly positive about *Read On!* The training, the effect of free choice on student and teacher motivation, the project's capacity to involve all learners and its non-traditional approaches to teaching and learning have all been praised. The following comment is typical of feedback from teachers on the programme.

> The most important aspect of the project has been the fact that it is based on the students' interests. They have had the opportunity to choose, experiment, and discover on their own. It has brought the class together as a group and it has enabled us as teachers to learn and experiment together with our students.

CATERINA MALFARÀ SACCHINI AND MICHELE CASTELLI, LICEO DES AMBROIS, OULX

2014–15 Impact study

In view of the quantity and quality of feedback on the programme, it was agreed that it would be useful to measure the impact of *Read On!* on Italian students and teachers in a formal evaluation. During the 2014–15 academic year, 120 teachers and 3,000 students from all over Italy participated in a mixed-methods research efficacy study. The research design included a variety of pre- and post-intervention evaluations as well as classroom observations, teacher and student interviews, and pre- and post-intervention questionnaires for all participants. The qualitative research was led by an independent academic researcher and quantitative data was compiled by cross-referencing results with two established tests from Oxford University Press and Lexile.

Why this works

Teachers, students, and parents in Italy all recognize the importance of good English skills for young people's futures. However, despite reforms, traditional and ineffective ways of teaching and learning are still the norm in Italy. *Read On!* encourages participants to see language learning in terms of choice, self-regulation, collaboration, and creativity rather than drills and testing. Day and Bamford (1998) assert that 'the most essential prerequisite for developing effective, efficient and independent second language readers through extensive reading has always been the individual committed teacher'. *Read On!* recruits teachers who are passionate about teaching and learning. It trains and supports them to transform their classrooms into self-starting communities of learners ready to experiment and explore language through reading, research, and presentation. This extensive reading initiative gives all participants the opportunity and resources to discover that freedom of choice and responsibility create successful life-long learners and citizens.

Glossary

Adaptation The retelling of a story or of an original novel in language graded to the readers' language level.

Affect An emotional state that may influence learning or behaviour.

Class readers A set of identical graded readers which all students in a class are working on at the same time.

CLIL (Content and Language Integrated Learning) A strategy for increasing the impact of foreign language teaching by combining it with the teaching of subjects like history, mathematics, or science.

Close reading Careful and analytical study of a text.

Cohesion The way in which sentences and phrases are linked to create connected text.

Collocation The way words are used together, as in 'heavy rain' (not *'strong rain').

Discourse A unit of speech or writing that is longer than a sentence.

Discourse marker A word or phrase used to separate sections of discourse.

Ellipsis The omission of words in writing or speech.

Extensive reading Reading a lot of easy texts for enjoyment, focusing on content and meaning, and developing confidence, fluency, and automaticity.

Graded materials Reading materials developed within a specific language range for students of different language competence.

Graded reader A narrative text written or adapted for second or foreign language learners.

Graphic organizer A page with a strong graphic design element which provides a framework for students to organize their work or thoughts in note form.

Headwords A word that forms a heading in a dictionary. It includes derived words, e.g. *go/goes/went/gone*. (See also *lexical syllabus*.)

Intensive reading Reading short, difficult texts, focusing on language, studying grammar use and rules, translating, using dictionaires.

L1 First language or mother tongue.

L2 Second or foreign language.

Language learner literature (LLL) Reading material specially written to help students to learn to read. The most common type of LLL is the graded reader.

Lexical syllabus A wordlist of headwords which beginner readers are expected to know at each level in a graded reader series. (See also *headwords*.)

Linguistic code The way the language of a text is structured, irrespective of its meaning.

Lockstep approach A classroom approach which requires all students to move forward at the same rate.

Process-based An approach which focuses on the learning steps taken by students over time, rather than on the end product of learning.

Readability formula A programme designed to assess what a reader can read, using the criteria of word and sentence lengths.

Reader response A reader's reaction, positive or negative, to a given text.

Reading circles Small groups of students who meet in the classroom to talk about the stories they have read.

Reading comfort zone The range of materials that learners can read easily and with confidence; the materials are well within a reader's linguistic competence.

Reading rate The number of words per minute that a reader can read and understand.

Reading target The requirement for students to read a given number of books in a given time.

Recognition vocabulary Words which students can understand in context when they read them but are not able to produce independently.

Redundancy The use of words that are not always necessary to clarify meaning.

Scaffolding Language support from peers, teacher, classroom set-up, or materials used to make a challenging task doable.

Scanning Reading a text quickly to find specific information.

SEN (Special Educational Needs) A way of describing students who have particular needs or differences which affect their ability to learn.

Sight vocabulary Words that readers recognize automatically, accurately, and every time, regardless of context.

Skimming Looking over a text quickly to get the general idea.

Sustained Silent Reading (SSR) Regular class time devoted to individual quiet reading.

Syntax The rules for constructing sentences in a language, for example, permissible word order.

Third-person narrative The telling of a story by a 'narrator', not by the main characters themselves.

Working memory Also known as 'short-term memory': the area of memory used for processing new information.

Useful websites

Chapter 1
http://www.readingmatrix.com/archives/archives_vol1_no1.html
http://nflrc.hawaii.edu/rfl/October2002/
http://nflrc.hawaii.edu/rfl/PastIssues/originalissues.html#131

Chapter 2
http://www.parisreview.com
http://www.guardian.co.uk/books
http://literature.britishcouncil.org/kazuo-ishiguro
http://www.philip-pullman.com
http://www.librarything.com

Chapter 4
https://elt.oup.com/cat/subjects/graded_reading/dominoes/

Chapter 5
https://elt.oup.com/teachers/bookworms/
http://www.oup-bookworms.com/teachers-only.cfm
https://elt.oup.com/student/bookwormsleveltest/

Chapter 6
https://elt.oup.com/teachers/bookworms/
https://elt.oup.com/teachers/readingcircles/

Chapter 9
http://www.shopbrodart.com
http://www.er-central.com/the-edinbugh-project-on-extensive-reading/
www.microvision.com

Chapter 10
http://moodlereader.org

Chapter 11
www.oup.com/elt/readon